The Real Jesus

Based On A True Story

by William Lucas

All rights reserved. No part of this book shall be reproduced or transmitted in any form or by any means, electronic, mechanical, magnetic, photographic including photocopying, recording or by any information storage and retrieval system, without prior written permission of the publisher. No patent liability is assumed with respect to the use of the information contained herein. Although every precaution has been taken in the preparation of this book, the publisher and author assume no responsibility for errors or omissions. Neither is any liability assumed for damages resulting from the use of the information contained herein.

Copyright © 2011 by William Lucas

ISBN 978-0-7414-7041-6

Printed in the United States of America

Published December 2011

INFINITY PUBLISHING
1094 New DeHaven Street, Suite 100
West Conshohocken, PA 19428-2713
Toll-free (877) BUY BOOK
Local Phone (610) 941-9999
Fax (610) 941-9959
Info@buybooksontheweb.com
www.buybooksontheweb.com

DEDICATION

I dedicate this book to the seekers of the world; that they may take comfort in knowing that Jesus loves us all. I made the statement in my previous book "*Journey to Life*" that Jesus is the creator of our local universe. To prove my statement, I ask the reader to look in the *Bible* at John 1:10 where it states: *"He was in the world and the world was made by him, and the world knew him not."* The world didn't recognize him as the creator of our local universe; and they still don't.

ACKNOWLEDGMENT

My thanks go out to Rebekah Pierce of Average Girl Magazine Richmond, Virginia, for the great job she did editing my manuscripts. And I am grateful to my sister Dolores for always being a good friend and for reading my manuscript and giving me valuable feedback. Besides, she said I couldn't publish it until she checked it out anyway (smile). I asked my sister Dolores what did she think about December 2012, did she think it will be the end of the world? She said she tell all her friends; if they don't get a call on their cell phone from God saying it will be the end of the world, don't worry about it. Sound advice. I also want to thank my neighbor, Beverly Bendrick, for reading my manuscript and providing good information in making my book more informative. Also, I want to thank Cheryll Weis and Jan Haddon of Unity Church of Bon Air in Richmond, Virginia for their help.

TABLE OF CONTENTS

Introduction 1
    The Inception of Christianity 2

Chapter 1 – The Real Jesus 9
    The Bestowal of Michael on Urantia 13
    Further Counsel and Advice 15
    The Times of Michael's Incarnation 17
    Jews and Gentiles..20
    Joseph and Mary 23
    Gabriel Appears to Elizabeth 24
    Joseph's Dream 27
    Jesus Earth Parents...29
    The Home at Nazareth 31
    The Trip to Bethlehem 32
    The Birth of Jesus 33
    The Presentation in the Temple......................36
    Herod Acts 38
    The Early Years of Jesus................................39
    Back in Nazareth...41
    The Seventh Year A.D. 1 47

Chapter 2 – The School Days 50
    The Twelfth Year (A.D. 6)..............................56
    Jesus at Jerusalem 58
    The Two Crucial Years 61
    Jesus' Fourteenth Year (A.D. 8) 62

Chapter 3 – The Death of Joseph 64
    The Fifteenth Year (A.D. 9)..............................66
    The Sermon in the Synagogue 69
    The Financial Struggle 70
    The Seventeenth Year (A.D. 11)......................73
    Rebecca the Daughter of Ezra.........................76
    The Later Adult Life of Jesus...........................79
    The Human Jesus 81
    On the Way to Rome..82
    An Analysis of Jonah 83
    The Caravan Trip to the Caspian Sea...............87

Chapter 4 – John the Baptist 91
    John Becomes a Nazarite 92
    The Baptism of Jesus 94
    The Forty Days...96

Chapter 5 – The Wedding at Cana...................101
    God's Wrath...106
    The Purpose of Affliction...............................108
    The Discourse on True Religion 110
    Resurrection of Lazarus 112

Chapter 6 – The Last Days Of Jesus 116
    Early Home Life...117
    Judas and the Chief Priest 120
    After the Noontime Meal 125
    On the Way to the Last Supper 127
    Beginning the Supper......................................127

Wash the Apostles Feet...130
Last Words to the Betrayer 132
Establishing the Remembrance Supper.....................134
In Gethsemane...134
The Last Group Prayer 135
Alone in Gethsemane 138
The Betrayer and the Arrest of Jesus 139
The Father's Will..141
On the Way to the High Priest Palace.......................147
Examination by Annas..148
Peter in the Courtyard 151
Before the Sanhedrin Court..153
The Hour of Humiliation..156
Second Meeting of the Court 157
The Private Examination by Pilate............................160
Jesus Before Herod 162
Pilate's Last Appeal...166
Pilate's Last Interview...168
Pilate Tragic Surrender 170
Just Before the Crucifixion 170
The End of Judas Iscariot..171

Chapter 7 – The Burial of Jesus 174
Meaning of the Death on the Cross...........................178
The Morontia Transit 181

Glossary..185

INTRODUCTION

Since the dawn of civilization, humankind has pondered the purpose of their existence on this planet. We stand in awe of this speck of dust that we call our Earth flying through space at tremendous speed in comparison with the vastness of the universe. We look toward the sky in the hopes of finding something conducive to this understanding. Some give up early in life. In disgust, they try to extirpate those thoughts from their minds only to find vestiges of those thoughts hounding them wherever they wander. They allowed their minds to be molded early in life, limiting their states of consciousness not realizing that not knowing the purpose of existence is what's causing most of their frustration, pain and sorrow. By limiting themselves, some people are not able to solve some of their more advanced problems; they don't make the connection that it is due to the limitations they have imposed upon themselves. You hear them cry-out: "Give me that old time religion that was good enough for my mother and father and is good enough for me." Sure it was good enough for our ancestors. But our ancestors didn't have the problems that our civilization has today. If they would only allow a little shift in consciousness, it would make a big difference in the quality of their lives. In their frustration, they are constantly looking for mundane substitutes, but the more they gain, the more they find themselves glutting for more. They have no peace in their souls.

The Inception of Christianity

From the time the emperor Constantine "Romanized" Christianity, its face has never been the same; there has been great violence surrounding it. Many Christians' beliefs changed during the time Constantine convened the council of Nicene in 325 A.D. when many of the important doctrines of the Catholic Church were adopted. A great many people of the Christian world today does not understand that many of the beliefs of the Christians world were adopted during this period of time and had nothing to do with Christ; this was the beginning of the Christian Bible. Constantine became a Christian because it benefited him politically; it had nothing to do with spirituality. The groups that clung more to the teachings of Christ were branded heretics; one of these groups was known as Gnostics; groups like this were tortured by the so-called Christians and forced underground until they died out, they were considered heretics.

Another Emperor who had a great influence on the distorted teachings of Christianity was Theodosius 1. He issued laws that were aimed at people who rejected the doctrine that was created by the Nicene Council. He made Christianity the official religion of the state, forcing many so called pagan temples to close. Theodosius was one of the Emperors who did the greatest disservice to humanity by completing the destruction of one of our greatest inheritances; he destroyed the Alexandrian library. This library contained records from all over the world—priceless records on science, religion and many other subjects; records that were accumulated over hundreds of years were destroyed. Those records, I'm sure, would have helped to solve the chaos in the history of the world's religions through the years; perhaps with those records we would have unraveled the problem of why man is on this planet.

After the evilness of those Emperors, there came another menace to civilization, the Emperor Justinian. He established the death penalty against what he called the heretics and pagans. It is said that in one area alone there were one hundred thousand people murdered so that he could rush the establishment of the Christian Orthodoxies. This was the foundation that the Christian world was built on, by the so-called Christian fathers. After that, there was the crusade, the so-called Holy War against Moslems to take Jerusalem with the blessing of Pope Urban II around 1,100 AD. Thousands were slaughtered; Christian factions started slaughtering Jews in Europe; the atrocities that were allowed during the crusade were unbelievable. There also was the Inquisition during the 13th Century that had Europe in social and economic chaos. Everyone was afraid to say anything against the church, afraid of being branded a heretic and severely punished for crimes against the church. The Inquisition was initiated under Pope Innocent IV; the Roman Catholic Church was also involved in "Burning at the Stake." At its inception, the Roman Catholic Church was the epitome of evil, and all of Christianity is based on the Roman Catholic Doctrine. How could God sanction such outrageous behavior?

That great Son of God, Jesus the Christ, warned if the house is not built on a sound foundation, it will not stand (Luke 6:47-48). In Psalm 127, it states: *"Except the Lord build the house they labor in vain that build it."* It may take years for it to tumble; all of Christianity will not stand on the foundation it was built on. I believe it was because of the foundation the Christian Church was built on; slavery in America was so cruel and allowed to last so long. I often wondered how concepts as cruel as hell get into the *Bible*. But after learning how the early Christian Church developed, I understood. Since the early Christian Church was established on cruelty, they projected that cruelty onto God. They literally forced people to do God's will with their hell and damnation. Have you ever wondered how many people's lives have been destroyed because of the hell and damnation concepts? People were not strong enough to live up to such strict rules, but they wanted to do God's will; it seems everything they enjoyed doing was a sin. Those so-called church fathers couldn't live up to those stringent rules themselves. Many sincere people became sick. They felt unworthy not being able to love God and do his will.

Hell started out as an allegory it was intended to help people visualize what life would be like with-out God. The so called Father of the early Christian era, started to use it as a means to control people. If we are not willing to do God's will; then we will go to what Revelation (20:14) call the second death. Our state of conscious will be annihilated.

(Proverbs 23:7) states "For as he thinketh in his heart so is he." People think about loving God and doing his will in one minute, and then the next minute there is the fear of going to hell if they don't. There is a great distorting of vibration here. This is why some prayers are not being answered. The thought of hell and damnation distort the good energy patterns. God Loves his creation there could be no such thing as hell in his universe.

The Christian Church claims that every man, woman and child has free will. But here's the catch: if you don't do God's will, you'll go to hell and burn for eternity. I'd call that forced will. The early Christian Church, as it was established, did everything by force.

As I mentioned above hell started out as an allegory to help people visualize what it would be like without the glory of God. Sometime during the years they were putting their control system in place, the churches realized they could use it as a control mechanism. And throughout the years, it has been blown out of proportion. In God's universe, there could not be such a state. We see or hear of many cruel things happening on Earth, but to burn for eternity is the ultimate cruelty. We are truly God's creation and He loves us; do you think He would allow something like hell to exist in his universe?

The Real Jesus

People of the earth, let us get real and let those things conjured up during the early establishment of the Christian Churches stay there. Let us not linger in the time warp of our ancient ancestors' past. The *Bible* states in Proverbs 23:7: "*For as he thinketh in his heart so is he.*" As we think of going to hell, we conjure up that state in our lives. Think positively and see if your life doesn't change for the better. We can create better states of existence for ourselves, but it takes time to overcome and master. It doesn't happen over night. You have to change all those negative vibrations you have accumulated throughout the years. People continue to suffer because they continue to ignore the reason for their existence; they continue to act in a way that distorts the vibration around them, that some call the human aura—when their action and their thoughts are flawed, this distorts the human aura and this, in turn, affects the cells in the human body. How do you think cancer is created in the body?

If we don't feed our souls by taking in spiritual nourishment, the soul becomes disoriented; the contentment of the soul brings happiness and a sense of well-being.

One of the biggest problems hindering us from expanding our spirituality is our continuous need to focus on the secular and not enough on the spiritual. For example, the Catholic Church has the mundane rule that to be a priest or nun, one has to be celibate, like God is concerned whether we abstain from sexual intercourse or not; what we should be focusing on loving our neighbor as ourselves. [Since the big sex scandal of the 1990's] I hope the Catholic Church realize it is dangerous to try to completely suppress the natural forces of nature; [she will just rear her head in some other form as has been demonstrated in the sex perversion]. Those priests' sex perversion didn't just start; this has been going on for years. In my autobiography, *Hard Times Don't Last Always,* I wrote how a priest approached me over 50 years ago when I was a child. He tried to lure me into bed with him. I described the devastating effect it had on me as a young boy. I believe those priests and nuns should be allowed to get married if that is their desire.

I hope no one misconstrues my intent. I am not advocating that people leave the churches, but we do need a little shift in consciousness. Humankind is better off because of Christianity; it was those sincere believers in Christ who have done a world of good, not those who were in it for power or prestige. Sadly, this is true of all the world's religions. In those different world religions, you'll find leaders of great knowledge, but very little understanding. It is usually the average people who give life to those religions. There is a book titled, *Why Christianity Must Change or Die.* The author, John Shelby Spong, was at the time he wrote the book Episcopal (Anglican) Bishop of Newark, New Jersey; he brings out the many problems of the Christian Churches, such as the cruelty of their foundation.

If people would examine a book called The Nag Hammadi Library; in December 1945 a set of 52 religious and philosophical texts, hidden in an earthenware jar for 1,600 years was accidentally unearthed. Some of texts tells the story about Jesus and his early followers. In these texts you will see how much the early writing about Jesus has changed. Some people will bet their last dime that the Bible is God's word and hasn't been temper with. This book is hard proof that there has been many changes.

If a sincere person would just read the history of the foundation of the Christian Churches they would wonder, as I had, how those churches could understand anything about the truth after all of their evilness. Jesus said the truth will set you free. That is one of the reasons most peoples' prayers are not answered because they do not understand the truth. That which they believe is partial-truth built on the wrong foundation. In Revelation 3:15, it states: *"I know thy works, that thou art neither cold nor hot: I would thou wert cold or hot."* I used to wonder why some people prayed and prayed and nothing happened. These people appeared to be sincere.

Now I understand what they believed to be true is not true; therefore, they are in the wrong vibration. Their truth was built on the wrong information. They are not able to receive the full affects of the Holy Spirit Jesus promised he'd send; their vibration prevents it. It's time to search for the truth and be set free. *"And ye shall know the truth, and the truth will make you free"* John 8:32.

I made the statement in my previous book "*Journey to Life"* that Jesus is the creator of our local universe. To prove my statement I ask my reader to look in the *Bible* at John 1:10 where it states: *"He was in the world and the world was made by him, and the world knew him not."* The world didn't recognize him as the creator of our local universe; and they still don't. Can it get any clearer than that; it states Jesus made the world and that was long before he incarnated into our world as Jesus the Christ. Our universe is the kingdom he mentions in John 18:36 "My kingdom is not of this world." These very high Sons of God are the ones I believe God were talking to in the *Bible* when it stated, *"And God said: Let us make man in our image, after our likeness"* Genesis 1:26. Jesus is one of those Creator Sons God was talking to long before his last initiation on our planet. You can read about these Creator Sons in "Journey to Life." www.buybooksontheweb.com. 877-289-2665 .

I know the academia must be whispering among themselves that I don't have a theological degree; therefore, I don't have the authority to write on such subjects as a true story of Jesus. But God gave me the authority to do His will, so I write (smile).

CHAPTER 1

The Real Jesus

Long before I knew of the existence of *The Urantia Book*, I wondered why Higher Beings such as angels didn't glean a history about our planet and give it to use now that portions of mankind are a little more civilized. But after reading the 2089 pages of *The Urantia Book*, I was convinced they had. I was amazed and shocked at the knowledge contained in the book. I couldn't understand why the academia didn't understand it. Now after studying on the nature of man, I realize that we are not as intelligent as we think we are.

Let me explain to you, the reader, a little about *The Urantia Book*. It appears to have the complete story of the history of our planet earth and far beyond. Only, their stories are not like our traditional stories; their stories are shockers. In my previous book, *Journey to Life,* I wrote about their version of the history of our planet in detail. When I first started reading *The Urantia Book*, I was like everyone else; because of its size I was intimidated, so I started off by reading the parts I was familiar with such as the story of Adam and Eve, the life and teachings of Jesus and the likes. Somewhere in the book, I read that one wouldn't understand the book unless you read it cover to cover; it was constructed that way. There is such great information in the book; I figured I had nothing to lose. I was working at the time, so it took me almost a year to complete it. I tried to analyze every section of the book trying to figure out if the information could be true. After reading the entire book, I was awe-stroked. I knew then that somehow this book was given to mankind by a higher source. During the time I read the book for the first time, I had been studying different religious concepts most of my adult life (I was sixty when I found *The Urantia Book*). I knew through my many years of studying that man could not have produced a book of that nature without help from higher a source.

I tried to find out who was responsible for publishing *The Urantia Book* and I learned Dr. William Sadler had it published in 1955. The academia tried everything they could think of during that period to identify the person who had actually written it. To this day, *The Urantia Book* has no known human author. But, again, because of the book's contents, I had little concern about who wrote the book because I was convinced man alone didn't write it.

Because of the distortion in the foundation of the Christian Church, the average person knows very little about the real Jesus Christ; for years we have been led down a rugged road, with no real purpose. I have felt since I was sixteen years old and a priest tried to lure me into bed with him that something was wrong with the way we practiced Christianity, but I was too young then to understand.

I had searched for many years to find answers; when I found *The Urantia Book* at age sixty, although I was grateful I found the book, I was also upset and wondered why it had taken so long. That was the first time I heard a little voice you sometimes hear people talking about whispering in my ear saying, "You wasn't ready yet." I questioned no more. It took me around five years to understand exactly what the little voice was saying; very few people seem to be able to grasp the real meaning of *The Urantia Book* and I needed certain life experience before I could understand the real meaning behind the book.

Has anyone given thought to the idea that Jesus was extremely intelligent for His age? The time he recruited His apostles, He was about the same age they were, in their mid or late 20's or early 30's. And there nothing to indicate He

The Real Jesus

had a better education. Yet his understanding and intelligence was far above theirs.

How many times did He mention He came to do the Father's will that His kingdom was not of this world? John 18:36. That is an indication He was once head of a kingdom. According to *The Urantia Book*, His kingdom is our universe. And it appears that everything He did on earth showed He was expecting to return to His kingdom.

The Urantia Book claims Jesus is one of many Creator Sons of God that is known in the higher worlds as Christ Michael—the one that the *Bible* calls Archangel Michael, but he is not an archangel. These Sons have to go through seven initiations before they can become sovereign of the universe they and their many helpers created. When Jesus came to earth, that was His seventh and final initiation.

The Creator Sons of God I mentioned are the rulers of the local universes of time and space. These universe creators were brought into being by God the Father and God the Son of the Trinity. Each of these Sons is the "Only-begotten Son" and there are about half a billion of them. They are called the "Only begotten" because they are the first brought into being after the trinity. These Sons are considered an order and are known as Michaels. Just as we have earthly parents, we also have creator parents. These Creator Sons have complimentary opposites that helped them build their universes and are known in the higher worlds as Universe Spirit Mothers. They are our spiritual parents, and God is the Father of us all. That is one reason why Jesus is also known as our older brother. He came into being billions of years before us. Jesus was known in the higher worlds after His last initiation as Christ Michael. He and his complimentary opposite are the Gods of our universe; that is one reason why we sometimes refer to Jesus as God. But He is not the Universal Father. These Sons are the ones I believe God were talking to in the *Bible* when it mentioned, *"And*

God said: Let us make man in our image, after our likeness" Genesis 1:26.

The different sections in *The Urantia Book* are not called chapters; they are called papers, and there are 196 papers in the book. It is stated in the book on page 1321:

"These groups of paper were sponsored by a commission of twelve Urantia midwayers acting under the supervision of a Melchizedek Revelatory Director. The basis of this narrative was supplied by a secondary midwayer who was at one-time assigned to the superhuman whatchcare of the apostle Andrew." [1]

The midwayers are an order of beings midway between angels and humans; they live on our planet, but in another dimension. We sometimes mistake them for angels when they are helping us. Melchizedeks are another order of Higher Beings; there are about ten million of them in our local universe. They are dispatched to worlds that have need of them. One of them visited our world during the time of Abraham; in the higher worlds, he is known as Machiventa and he stayed on our earth for almost one hundred years. In the *Bible,* he is said to be without mother or father and without descent; in other words, he was from another world Hebrew 7:3. But before going any further, Urantia means earth to the Higher Beings. Therefore, *The Urantia Book* is a book that tells the story of our earth.

The Melchizedek director of revelatory commission said this was the occasion when Immanuel presented to Michael the charge of his seventh initiation commission; this initiation counseling of Immanuel to Michael who is the local universe ruler and subsequently became Jesus of Nazareth on earth. According to *The Urantia Book,* Immanuel is an older brother of Michael; in the higher worlds, he was the one that counseled Michael before taking off on his final initiation and incarnation. While Michael (Jesus Christ) was taking care of business on earth, Immanuel and Gabriel took charge of our local universe.

The Bestowal of Michael on Urantia

ASSIGNED by Gabriel to supervise the restatement of the life of Michael when on Urantia and in the likeness of mortal flesh, I, the Melchizedek director of the revelatory commission entrusted with this task, am authorized to present this narrative of certain events which immediately preceded the Creator Son's arrival on Urantia to embark upon the terminal phase of his universe bestowal experience. To live such identical lives as he imposes upon the intelligent beings of his own creation, thus to bestow himself in the likeness of his various orders of created beings, is a part of the price which every Creator Son must pay for the full and supreme sovereignty of his self-made universe of things and beings.

Before the events I am about to delineate, Michael of Nebadon had bestowed himself six times after the similitude of six differing orders of his diverse creation of intelligent beings. Then he prepared to descend upon Urantia in the likeness of mortal flesh, the lowest order of his intelligent will creatures, and, as such a human of the material realm, to execute the final act in the drama of the acquirement of universe sovereignty in accordance with the mandates of the divine Paradise Rulers of the universe of universes.

In the course of each of these preceding bestowals Michael not only acquired the finite experience of one group of his created beings, but he also acquired an essential experience in Paradise cooperation which would, in and of itself, further contribute to constituting him the sovereign of his self-made universe. At any moment throughout all past local universe time, Michael could have asserted personal sovereignty as a Creator Son and as a Creator Son could have ruled his universe after the manner of his own choosing. In such an event, Immanuel and the associated Paradise Sons would have taken leave of the universe. But Michael did not wish to rule Nebadon merely in his own isolated right, as a Creator Son. He desired to ascend through actual experience in co-operative subordination to the Paradise Trinity to that high place in universe status where he would become qualified to rule his universe and administer its affairs with that perfection of insight and wisdom of execution which will sometime be characteristic of the exalted rule of the Supreme Being. He aspired not to perfection of rule as a Creator Son but to supremacy of administration as the embodiment of the universe wisdom and the divine experience of the Supreme Being.

Michael, (Jesus) therefore, had a double purpose in the making of these seven bestowals upon the various orders of his universe creatures: First, he was completing the required experience in creature understanding which is demanded of all Creator Sons before they assume complete sovereignty. At any time a Creator Son may rule his universe in his own right, but he can rule as the supreme representative of the Paradise Trinity only after passing through the seven universe-creature bestowals. Second, he was aspiring to the privilege of representing the maximum authority of the Paradise Trinity which can be exercised in the direct and personal administration of a local universe. Accordingly, did Michael, during the experience of each of his universe bestowals, successfully and acceptably voluntarily subordinate himself to the variously constituted wills of the diverse associations of the persons of the Paradise Trinity. That is, on the first bestowal he was subject to the combined will of the Father, Son, and Spirit; on the second bestowal to the will of the Father and the Son; on the third bestowal to the will of the Father and the Spirit; on the fourth bestowal to the will of the Son and the Spirit; on the fifth bestowal to the will of the Infinite Spirit; on the sixth bestowal to the will of the Eternal Son; and during the seventh and final bestowal, on Urantia, to the will of the Universal Father.[2]"
The Paradise Trinity is Father, Son and Holy Spirit; they are real personalities of paradise, the center of all things.

One of the main reasons Jesus chose our planet as His last initiation, was due to the past history of our planet: the rebellion of the prince of this world along with Lucifer. He mentioned in John 12:31 *"Now is the judgment of this world: now shall the prince be cast out."* Also, we have the fall of Adam and Eve. Because of these two incidents, our planet was going to the dogs. It was due to these two occurrences, that our planet earth (the higher ones call Urantia) was way behind in its spiritual evolution. Jesus, being our spiritual father, loved us and longed to do something to correct our disruptive past. He knew it would take hundreds of years after His initiation on our planet to show any improvements. In my previous book, *Journey to Life,* I go into details about how these two incidents disrupted the spiritual evolution of our planet. This is the reason we have had so much discord on our planet. Perhaps after the year 2012, the end of the Mayan Calendar when new spiritual energy starts bombarding our planet, life on earth will change for the better.

Further Counsel and Advice

As Michael prepared to leave for Urantia from that far distance local universe headquarters, Immanuel gave Michael some sound advice. He counseled Michael regarding the general conduct, saying to Michael, *"Allow me to give certain advices that have been reached in consultation with Gabriel that concerns minor phases of your mortal life. We further suggest:*

1. *"That in pursuit of the ideal of your mortal life, you also give some attention to the realization and exemplification of some things practical and immediately helpful to your fellow man.*

2. *As concerns family relationship, give precedence to the accepted customs of family life as you find them established in the day and generation of your bes-*

towal. Live your family and community life in accordance with the practices of the people among whom you have elected to appear.

3. *In your relation to the social order we advise that you confine your efforts largely to spiritual regeneration and intellectual emancipation. Avoid all entertainments with the economic-structure and political commitments of your day. More especially devote yourself to living the ideal religious life on Urantia.*

4. *Under no circumstances and not even in the least details, should you interfere with the normal and orderly progressive evolution of the Urantia races. But this prohibition must not be interpreted as limiting your efforts to leave behind you on Urantia an enduring and improved system of positive religious ethics. As a dispensational Son, you are granted certain privileges pertaining to the advancement of spiritual and religious states of the world peoples.*

5. *As you may see fit, you are to identify yourself with existing religious and spiritual movements as you may find on Urantia, but in every possible manner seek to avoid the formal establishment of an organized cult, crystallized religion, or a segregated ethical grouping of human beings. Your life and teachings are to become the common heritage of all religions and all peoples.*

6. *To the end that you may not unnecessarily contribute to the creation of subsequent stereotyped systems of Urantia religious beliefs or other types of non-progressive religious loyalties, we advise you still further: Leave no writings behind you on the planet. Refrain from all writing, upon permanent materials; enjoin your associates to make no images or other likeness of yourself in the flesh. See*

that nothing potentially idolatrous is left on the planet at the time of departure.

7. *While you will live the normal and average social life of the planet, being a normal individual of the male sex, you will probably not enter the marriage relation, which relation will be wholly honorable and consistent with your bestowal; but I must remind you that one of the incarnation mandates of Sonorington (one of the seven sacred spheres of the Father) forbids the leaving of offspring behind on any planet by a bestowal Son of Paradise origin.* "[3]

The Times of Michael's Incarnation

Before we commence with the actual story of Jesus' life, we will take a peek at the times that surrounded his birth. During that time, the earth was experiencing a great revival of spiritual thinking and religious living that had not been seen in all its previous post-Adamic history; nor has it experienced anything since. When Michael incarnated on Earth the world presented a suitable condition for the Creator Son's bestowal as the environment at that time was very favorable. At that particular time the Greek culture and language spread over the Occident and part of the Orient, the Jew being Levantine in nature part Occidental and part Oriental was fitted to utilize such culture and linguistic for an effective spreading of a new religion east and west.

There was a favorable situation of political rule of the Mediterranean world by the Romans. This situation was very well illustrated by the activities of Paul, who was Hebrew in culture, but proclaimed the gospel of a Jewish Messiah in the Greek's tongue while he himself was a Roman citizen. At the birth of Christ, the entire Mediterranean was a unified empire. They had good roads for the first time in world history; these roads interconnected with many major centers.

The seas were free of pirates and a great age of trade and travel was taking place. (Europe did not enjoy another period of trade and travel such as that until nineteen century after Christ.) The majority of the people in the Greco-Roman world languished in poverty as a small upper class were rich. The miserable included the rank and file of humanity; there was no happy middle class in those days; it had just begun to make its appearance in Roman society.

Those Higher Beings claim that Jews were part of the older Semitic race that included the Babylonians, the Phoenicians and the Carthaginians during the beginning of the first century after Christ. The Jews were the most influential group of the Semitic people. They occupied a very strategic geographic position in the world. This geographic position was ruled and organized for trade. Much of the great highways joining the nation together passed through Palestine, which became the crossroad for those continents. The travel, trade, and armies of Babylonian, Assyria, Egypt, Syria, Greece, Parthia, and Roman passed through Palestine. Many, caravan routes from the Orient passed through some parts of this area on their way to the few good seaports at the eastern end of the Mediterranean where ships carried their cargoes to all parts the maritime Occident. And over half of caravan traffic passed through or near the little town of Nazareth in Galilee.

Palestine was the home of Jewish religious culture, and also the birth place of Christianity. The Jewish people were all over the world in many nations and trading in every province of the Roman and Parthian. But the Greeks were the ones that provided the language and culture. The Roman's built the roads and unified the empire. The dispersion of the Jews with their over two hundred synagogues, organized religious communities that were scatted here and there throughout the Roman Empire, they provided the culture centers. Here is where the new gospel of the kingdom of heaven found its initial acceptance and which eventually spread all over the world.

At that time, the Jewish synagogue allowed other border believers "devout" and "God fearing men" to hold teachings along the outer synagogue; it was among this group that Paul made most of his early converts to Christianity. Even the temple at Jerusalem had a court for the Gentiles. In fact, it was at Antioch the capital of ancient Syria, that Paul's disciples were first called "Christians."

The centralizing of the Jewish temples at Jerusalem is the secret of the survival of monotheism, and hopeful nurturing and sending forth to the world a new and enlarged concept of the one God of all nations and Father of all mortals. This temple service at Jerusalem represents the survival of religious plus cultural concepts.

The Jews of this period, although somewhat under Roman rule, enjoyed an unbelievable amount of self-government, and they, remembering the only recent attempt of deliverance that was executed when Judas Maccabee in 175-174 B.C., waged a successful revolt against the Syrians. The Jewish people were roused in expectation of still a greater deliverer, the long expected Messiah.

Palestine's secret to survival as the kingdom of the Jews, a semi-independent, state was because of the Roman foreign policy to maintain control of Palestinians and their travels between the Orient and the Occident; the Romans did not want any power to rise in the Levant which would attempt to curb any of their expanding in this area.

The Jews were unusually leery and suspicious during the time of Jesus because they were then ruled by an outsider, Herod, who had seized the overlord-ship of Judea by cleverly scheming to gain favor of the Roman rulers. Herod professed loyalty to the Hebrew ceremonial observance and he then built temples to many strange gods. The cozy relation between Herod and the Roman rulers made the world a safe place for Jewish travelers. They traveled over the distant places of the Roman Empire and foreign treaty nations, proclaiming the gospel of the kingdom of heaven. Herod built the harbor at Caesarea that further aided in making Palestine the crossroad of the civilized world. He died in 4 B.C.

His son Herod Antipas governed Galilee and Perea during Jesus' youth and ministry to A.D. 39. Antipas like his father, was a great builder; he rebuilt many of the cities of Galilee, including the important trade center of Sapphoris. However the Galileans were not regarded with full favor by Jerusalem's religious leaders and rabbinical teachers. Galilee was more Gentile than Jew when Jesus was born.

Jews and Gentiles

At the time of Jesus, the Jews had already reached a conclusion as far as their origin, history and destiny was concerned. They had in place a rigid wall of resistance between themselves and the Gentile world. At that time, they looked upon the Gentiles with utter contempt. They worshiped the letter of their law; they also engaged in self-righteousness based upon the false pride of their descendants. They indulged in preconceived ideas concerning the promise Messiah envisaged, a Messiah who would come as a part of their national and racial history, which was a false history to start with.

The teachings of Jesus concerning tolerance and kindness were against the long-standing practice of the Jews toward other people whom they considered heathen. For years, the Jews harbored a fixed attitude towards the outside world, which made it impossible for them to accept Christ's teachings concerning the spiritual brotherhood of man. They were unwilling to share Yahweh on equal terms with the Gentiles and were also unwilling to accept as the Son of God one who taught such strange teachings.

The scribes, the Pharisees and the priesthood held the Jews in a terrible bondage of ritualism and legalism that was much more real than the Roman rules. The Jew of Jesus' day were not only held captive to the laws, but also equally bound by the fetter of traditions that involved and invaded every aspect of their personal and social lives. It's sad how some people allow tradition to enslave their minds, as though their ancestors were living through them; they are not free to express their own livingness. And many today are doing the same thing; tradition has them enslaved.

The many regulations of conduct had a firm grip on every loyal Jew, as though they were possessed. It is not strange that they rejected one of their own, who presumed to ignore their sacred tradition and had the audacity to be indifferent to their honored rules of social conduct. They would not look upon one who did not hesitate to butt head with dogmas they regarded as having been decreed by Abraham himself. Moses gave them their laws and they would not compromise.

By the first century after Christ, the spoken interpretation of the laws by those recognized Hebrew teachers and scribes had become a higher authority than the written laws itself. This made it easier for those certain religious leaders of the Hebrews to turn people against accepting any new gospel. The situation made it impossible for the Jews to fulfill their divine destiny as messengers of the new gospel of religious freedom and spiritual liberty. They could not break the shackles of tradition. In fact, just before the actual papers on Jesus, the midwayer that sponsored those papers intervened and said.

[*"In carrying out my commission to restate the teachings and retell the doings of Jesus of Nazareth, I have drawn freely upon all sources of record and planetary information. My ruling motive has been to prepare a record which will not only be enlightening to the generation of men now living, but which may also be helpful to all future generations.*

From the vast store of information made available to me, I have chosen that which is best suited to the accomplishment of this purpose. As far as possible I have derived my information from purely human sources. Only when such sources failed, have I resorted to those records which are superhuman. When ideas and concepts of Jesus' life and teachings have been acceptably expressed by a human mind, I invariably gave preference to such apparently human thought patterns. Although I have sought to adjust the verbal expression the better to conform to our concept of the real meaning and the true import of the Master's life and teachings, as far as possible, I have adhered to the actual human concept and thought pattern in all my narratives. I well know that those concepts which have had origin in the human mind will prove more acceptable and helpful to all other human minds. When unable to find the necessary concepts in the human records or in human expressions, I have next resorted to the memory resources of my own order of earth creatures, the midwayers. And when that secondary source of information proved inadequate, I have unhesitatingly resorted to the superplanetary sources of information] Acknowledgment; page134, paper121.

At the beginning of paper 122, the midwayer that presented it said it would be difficult to explain, the different reasons Palestine was selected for Michael bestowal and especially as to the reason why the family of Joseph and Mary were selected as parents of the Son of God on earth.

After Michael (Jesus) studied the special report of the status of segregated worlds prepared by the Melchzedeks, in counsel with Gabriel, Lord Michael finally chose Urantia as the planet to act out his final initiation. Before this decision was final, Gabriel made a personal visit to earth, and as a result of his study of human groups and survey of spiritual, intellectual, racial, and geographic features of the world and it's people, his decision was that the Hebrews possessed the quality at that time that qualified them for the selection as the bestowal race. At Michael's approval of this decision Gabriel dispatched to earth the family commission of twelve-selected from the higher orders of the universe personalities, which were trusted with the task of making a study of Jewish family life. When the commission finished their job, Gabriel was on earth (in another dimension) and received the report, which nominated three different union of Jewish families as being in the opinion of the commission, equally suited as bestowal families for Michael intended incarnation. From the three couples chosen, Gabriel made the personal choice of Joseph and Mary; afterward he made an individual appearance to Mary at which time he told her the good news, that she been selected to become the earth mother of the bestowal child.

As I read this story, I was amazed at the work that goes on behind the scene that we do not have the slightest awareness of. We act as though things happen in the spiritual realm by chance or some magic connotation. Very few of us ever consider the preparation that goes on for things to manifest in our world.

Joseph and Mary

Joseph was the human father of Jesus; as a Hebrew, he carried non-Jewish racial strains which were added to his ancestry tree from time to time by the female line of his progenitors. The ancestry of Jesus' father went all the way back to Abraham and through this patriarch to the earlier line of his ancestors leading to the Sumerians and Nodites, and through the southern tribes of the ancient blue man, Cro-Magnon man, to Andon and Fonta. David and Solomon were not in the direct line of Joseph's ancestry; neither did Joseph's lineage go directly back to Adam. Joseph's direct ancestors were mechanics, builders, carpenters, masons, and smiths. He was a carpenter and later a contractor. His family was from a long line of important nobility and common people.

Mary the mother of Jesus was a descendant of a long line of novel ancestors, many of whom were the most remarkable women of Earth's history. Although Mary was considered average for her times with a normal temperament, her family tree included women like Bathsheba, Ruth, Ratta, and Eve. No Jewish woman of that time had a more illustrious linage of common and famous ancestors or one extending back to more favorable beginning. Mary's ancestors, like Joseph's, were characterized by strange, but average people; also numerous outstanding personalities showed every now and then in the march toward civilization and progressive evolution of religion. In terms of race, it is not proper to regard Mary as a Jew. In terms of culture, she was a Jew, but in hereditary she was a composite of Syrian, Hittite, Phoenician, Greeks, and Egyptian, stock. Her racial inheritance was more general than that of Joseph.

Out of all the couple that lived in Palestine at the time of Michael intended incarnation, Joseph and Mary possessed the most ideal combination of widespread racial connection and superior personality endowments. It was the plan of Jesus to appear on Earth as an average man that the common might understand and receive him; that is why Gabriel selected Joseph and Mary to be the bestowal parents.

Gabriel Appears to Elizabeth

Jesus work on Earth was started by John the Baptist. John's father, Zacharias, belonged to the Joseph priesthood his mother, Elizabeth, was a member of a more prosperous group of the same large family, a group which Jesus' mother Mary belonged. Zacharias and Elizabeth were married for many years, but had no children.

It was in the latter part of June B.C. 8, about three months after Mary and Joseph were married, that Gabriel

The Real Jesus

appeared to Elizabeth, and just as later he made an appearance to Mary, Jesus' mother. He said something to the effect, as your husband Zacharias, now stands before the alter in Jerusalem, and the people assembled and pray for the coming deliverer, I have come to announce you will shortly bear a son who will be a forerunner of this divine teacher, and you shall name him John. He will dedicate his life to God and when he grows-up you will find delight in him; he will turn souls to God. He shall also proclaim the coming of that one that will heal the souls of your people and the spirit liberator of all mankind. Your kin Mary will be the mother of this child and I will also appear to her."

This vision greatly frightened Elizabeth; after Gabriel left, she thought at length about this experience concerning her majestic visitor. She told no one about this revelation. For five months, Elizabeth kept the secret even from her husband. When she finally told the story to her husband, Zacharias, he was skeptical and for weeks doubted the entire experience until Elizabeth began to show. There was no question that his wife was expecting. Zacharias was very confused about Elizabeth impending motherhood, and he never doubted the integrity of his wife. But what bothered Zacharias was his advancing age; it was about six weeks before John was born when Zacharias had an impressive dream that really convinced him that Elizabeth was to become a mother of a child of destiny, one who was to prepare the way for the Messiah.

Gabriel appeared to Mary around the mid-point of November B.C. 8, while she was working in her Nazareth home. After Mary knew for sure that she was with child, she persuaded Joseph to let her journey to the city of Judah four miles west of Jerusalem in the hills to visit her cousin Elizabeth Gabriel had informed each of these mothers to-be of his appearance to the other, so naturally they wanted to get together to compare experiences. So Mary stayed at her distant cousin's for three weeks. Elizabeth helped to strengthen Mary's faith in Gabriel's vision; she was more dedicated to mothering the child of destiny whom she was soon to present to the world.

John was born in the city of Judah on March 25, 7 B.C. Zacharias and Elizabeth were very excited when the day came and Elizabeth truly bore a son just as Gabriel had promised. From his earliest infancy, John was impressed by his parents constantly reminding him that he would grow up to be a spiritual leader and spiritual teacher. As a child, he appeared constantly at the service of his father and was very impressed by the laws of the Jews.

One day around sundown, before Joseph got home, Gabriel appeared to Mary by the side of a low stone table, and after she had composed herself, he said: *"I come at the bidding of one who is my master and who you shall love and nurture. To you Mary, I bring glad tidings when I announced that the conception within you was ordained by heaven, and that in due time you will become the mother of a son; you shall call him Joshua, (Jesus) and he shall inaugurate the kingdom of heaven on earth and among men. Speak not of this matter save to Joseph and Elizabeth, your kinswoman, to whom I have also appeared, and who shall presently also bear a son whose name shall be John, and who will prepare the way for the message of the deliverance which your son shall proclaim to man with great power and deep conviction. And doubt not my word, Mary, for this home has been chosen as the mortal habitat of the child of destiny. My benediction rest upon you, the power of the most high will strengthen you, and the Lord of the earth shall over shadow you."[4]*

Mary pondered the visitation she had experienced for many weeks until she was sure she was with child, and before she dared to tell her husband about the strange event. When Joseph did hear the story about Mary's visitor, although he had great confidence in Mary, he was greatly troubled and was not able to sleep for many nights. In the beginning, Joseph had doubts. When he became convinced that Mary really had heard the voice and saw the form of a divine messenger, he was mentally confused, as he pondered how such a thing could be. How could an offspring of human beings be a child of destiny? Joseph was not able to reconcile with these confusing ideas that they, of all people, were chosen to become parents of the Messiah. It was the Jewish belief that the divine deliverer would be of divine nature. So as the parents of the expected divine reached this conclusion, Mary hastened to go visit with Elizabeth. (Gabriel's announcement to Mary came the day after the conception of Jesus, and it was the only event of supernatural occurrence connected with Mary's entire experience of carrying or bearing the child of destiny.)

Joseph's Dream

Joseph was not very happy about the idea of his wife, becoming the mother of a very exceptional child until he had a very impressive dream. In his dream, a stupendous celestial being appeared to him and said, among other things: *"Joseph, I appear by command of him who now reigns on high and I am directed to instruct you concerning the son Mary shall bear, and who will become a great light in the world. In him shall be light; and his life shall become the light of mankind. He will first come to his own people, but they will hardly receive him; but as many as receive him to them he will reveal that they are the children of God."*[5] After this dream, Joseph no longer had doubts about Gabriel visiting Mary and that the promised child was to become a divine messenger to the earth.

In these visitations, nothing was ever mentioned about the House of David; nothing was said about Jesus becoming the "deliverer of the Jews." Nothing was said about him being the long expected Messiah that the Jews had expected.

But he was the world deliverer. His mission was to all people, not to one group.

Joseph was not of the line of David; in fact, Mary had more of David's ancestry than he. Joseph went to the city of Bethlehem to be registered for the Roman census, was because six generations earlier, Joseph's paternal ancestors of that time, being an orphan, was adopted by one Zadoc, who was a direct descendant of David; that was the reason Joseph was consider of the house of David.

Many of the Messianic prophecies of the Old Testament were made to apply to Jesus long after he had lived on earth. For centuries, the Hebrew prophets prophesized the coming of the deliverer. I am sure that this came from the promise of Adam, Eve, and the Melchizedek, of their promise of a coming Son. But for the Jews, these promises were constructed by successive generations as referring to a new Jewish ruler who would sit upon the throne of David, and by some miraculous methods of Moses, proceed to establish the Jews in Palestine as a powerful nation free from foreign rulers. The Western World misapplied many Old Testament sayings to the life of Jesus, and many of them were distorted. For example, the passage were it mentions "that a maiden shall bear a son" was made to read *"A virgin shall bear a son."* This was true of the genealogies of both Mary and Joseph. Passages were rearranged so that it would seem to apply to Jesus' life. The distortions that went on during the so called Church Fathers time were unbelievable, creating their own belief and claiming it was inspired by God. The early followers of Jesus too often gave into the temptation to make all of the old prophetic sayings appear to have found fulfillment in the life of their Master, Jesus. Jesus himself at one time publicly denied any connection with the royal House of David.

The Real Jesus

Jesus Earth Parents

Here, I would like to familiarize my readers with some of the human traits of Jesus' mother and father. Joseph was a low keyed person, extremely conscious, and in every way faithful to the religious convictions and practice of his people. He didn't have too much to say, as, he was more of a thinker. The sorrowful experience of the Jewish people brought lots of sadness to his heart. When Joseph was young growing up with his eight brothers and sisters, he was more cheerful; he was rarely sad, but in the early years of his marriage life (during Jesus' childhood), he experienced mild spiritual discouragement. These temperamental modes of Joseph were greatly improved just before his untimely death and after his economic situation improved by his advancement from the ranks of carpenter to a well to-do contractor.

Mary's temperament, on the other hand, was opposite to that of her husband. She was usually cheerful, rarely depressed and possessed an ever-sunny disposition. She never seemed to be sorrowful until after her husband's death. She was hardly over this state of shock when the anxieties and questions of the extraordinary career of her oldest son were thrust upon her, which was rapidly unfolding before her astonished eyes. But throughout all of this unusual experience, Mary was composed, courageous and fairly wise in her relationship with her strange and little understood first born, and his surviving brothers and sisters. Sadly one of Jesus' brothers died when Jesus was young.

Jesus got quite a bid of his unusual gentleness and marvelous sympathetic understanding of human nature from his father; he inherited his gift as a great teacher and tremendous capacity for righteous indignation from his mother. Jesus was sometimes like his father—meditative and worshipful, sometimes characterized by sadness; but he went forward with his mother optimist and with a determined attitude. It seemed that Mary's attitude to dominate the divine Son as he grew up and swung into the momentous stride of adult life. From Joseph, Jesus obtained his strict training in the usage of the Jewish ceremonials and his unusual acquaintance with the Hebrew Scriptures; from Mary, he inherited a broader view point of religion and a more liberal concept of personal spiritual freedom.

Both of Jesus parents were well educated for their times. Joseph was a thinker; Mary a planner. Joseph's eyes were black and his hair was brunet; Mary was a brown-eyed blonde type. If Joseph had lived, longer he would have no doubt believed in the divine mission of his oldest son. Mary alternated between believing and doubting; she was greatly influenced by the position taken by her other children, relatives and friends. She was always steady in her final attitude by her remembrance of the appearance of Gabriel. Mary was an expert weaver and more skilled than the average householder in the art of home-keeping. In short, both Joseph and Mary were good teachers; they made sure their children were well versed in the learning of the times.

Joseph met Mary when he was a young man. He was employed by Mary's father in the work of building an addition to his house; it was when Mary brought Joseph a cup of water during the noon day meal that the courtship started off. This couple was destined, to be Jesus parents. At the time that they got married, Joseph was twenty-one. They married at Mary's house in the area of Nazareth. This was the conclusion of a normal courtship of almost two years duration, according to the custom. Right after marriage, they moved into their new home that Joseph built with the help of his two brothers.

The larger part of Joseph's family became a believer in Jesus, but very few of Mary's family believed in him until after his death. Joseph leaned more to the spiritual concept of the coming Messiah, where as Mary and her family, especially her father, clung to the idea of a temporal deliverer and political ruler. Mary's ancestors were identified as Maccabean (a political group of the time). Joseph held to the Eastern or Babylonian views of the Jewish religion, but Mary leaned more to the liberal, which was a broader view of the Western, or Hellenistic, understanding of the prophets.

The Home at Nazareth

Jesus home was not far from the high hills in the northerly part of Nazareth some distance from the village spring that was in the eastern part of town. He and his family lived on the outskirts of the city; this made it easier for Jesus to take strolls often to the countryside and to take trips up to the top of this nearby highland, the highest of all the hills of southern Galilee except the Mount Tabor range to the east and the hills of Nain that were around the same height.

Joseph and his family lived in a one room stone structure with a flat roof and an adjoining building to house the animals. The furniture included a low stone table, earthenware and stone dishes and pots, a lamp stand, several small stools and mats for sleeping on the stone floor. In the back yard close to the animal housing was the place that sheltered the oven and the mill for grinding grain. It took two people to operate this kind of mill: one to grind while the other feed the grinder. When Jesus was a small boy, he often fed the grinder while his mother turned the wheel. When the family grew in size they would all squat around the large stone table and enjoy their meals, helping themselves from a common dish or pot of food. In the winter, at the evening meal, the table was lighted by a small, flat, clay lamp filled with olive oil. After the birth of their daughter Martha, Joseph built an additional large room to the house that was used as a carpenter shop during the day and sleeping quarters at night.

The Trip to Bethlehem

In March B.C. 8, (the month Joseph and Mary married), Caesar Augustus ordered that all inhabitants of the Roman Empire should be counted so that a census could be made to be used for better taxation. But the Jews were always against any attempt to "numbering the people," in connection with serious domestic difficulties of Herod, King of Judea. He conspire the postponement of taking of census in the Jewish kingdom for one year. Throughout all the Roman Empire, the census was registered in the year B.C. 8, except in the Palestine kingdom of Herod where it was taken in B.C. 7, one year later.

It was not required for Mary to go to Bethlehem for enrollment. Joseph could register for her. But Mary being an adventurous and aggressive person demanded that she should. She feared being left alone; she might have the baby while Joseph was away and Bethlehem was not far away from the city of Judah. Mary was thinking of a visit with her kin Elizabeth. Joseph forbade Mary to go with him, but his forbidding was in vain. When the food was packed for three or four days, Mary prepared double portions and got ready for the journey. Joseph and Mary were poor; they only had one beast of burden. Mary being large with child, rode on the donkey with the food and supplies, while Joseph walked leading the animal. The building and furnishing of a house had been a strain on Joseph he also had to contribute to the support of his parents as his father was recently disabled. The couple left from their home early on the morning of August 18, B.C. 7, on their journey to Bethlehem.

The first day on their journey took them around the foothills of Mount Gilboa; there they camped for the night near the river Jordan; they speculated on what their son would be like, Joseph holding to the concept of a spiritual teacher, and Mary held to the idea of a Messiah, a deliverer of the Hebrew nation. Early the next morning, on August 19, they continued their journey. They ate their noonday meal at the foot of mount Sartaba overlooking the Jordan valley; they journeyed on making Jericho by night where they stopped at an inn on the outskirts of the city. After the evening meal they held a long discussion concerning the oppressiveness of the Roman rule, Herod's census enrollment and the influence of Jerusalem and Alexandria as center of Jewish training and culture. After this lengthy discussion, the couple retired for a night's rest.

At the crack of dawn on the morning of August 20, they continued their journey reaching Jerusalem before noon, visiting the Temple, then going on to their destination, arriving in Bethlehem at mid-afternoon. The inn they selected was overcrowded; Joseph tried to get lodging with distant relatives, but every room in Bethlehem was filled to capacity. They returned to the inn and were told that the caravan stables, hewn out of the side of a rock and situated right under the inn, had been cleared of animals and cleaned to accommodate lodgers. Joseph left the donkey in the courtyard, shouldered their bags of clothing and provisions, and with Mary, they walked down the stone steps to their lodging below. They found themselves situated in what used to be a grain storage room; to the front of the room was the stall and mangers (Tents were used as curtains); they considered themselves lucky to have such a comfortable room under such circumstances. Joseph wanted to go right out and enroll, but Mary was weary; she was distressed and asked him to stay by her side, which he did.

The Birth of Jesus

All that, night Mary was restless; they did not sleep much. At the break of day, pangs of childbirth were well in advance. At noon on August the 21, 7 B.C., with the help and kindness of fellow women travelers, Mary delivered a male child. Jesus of Nazareth was born into the world, wrapped in the cloths that Mary had brought with her with the thought in mind this might happen; she laid her son in a nearby manger. Jesus was the same as all babies born before him and all babies born after him. On the eighth day, Jesus was circumcised as required by Jewish law. He was formally named Joshua (Jesus).

The day after Jesus was born, Joseph went and enrolled. While enrolling, he met a man they had talked with two nights before. Joseph thought of him as a well-to-do person who had a room at the inn. After Joseph talked to him about his situation, the man was kind enough to let the couple have his room while he took the place that was used as a room on occasions, but was actually a granary. That afternoon, they moved up to the inn, and they stayed for almost three weeks until they found lodging at one of Joseph's distant relatives' home.

Two days after the birth of Jesus, Mary sent word to Elizabeth that she had given birth to a boy. Mary received word in return inviting Joseph up to Jerusalem to talk over current events with Zacharias. The following day, Joseph went to Jerusalem to visit with Zacharias. Zacharias and his wife were obsessed with the understanding that Jesus was to become the Jewish deliverer, the Messiah, and their son John was to be his chief of staff. It was not difficult for Zacharias and Elizabeth to talk Joseph into staying in Bethlehem, since his wife Mary had the same idea that Jesus would grow up to become the successor of David on the throne of Israel. The couple stayed in Bethlehem more than a year.

At noon the day that Jesus was born, the angels that were stationed on our planet did assemble under their director and they did sing songs of glory over the Bethlehem manger, but their songs of praise were not heard by humans ears; they were sung in another dimension. No shepherds came, nor did any other mortal creatures come to pay homage to the babe of Bethlehem until the day of the arrival of certain priests from Ur who were sent down from

Jerusalem by Zacharias. The priests from Mesopotamia were told by some strange religious teacher of their country that he had a dream; in the dream, he was informed that "the Light of Life" was about to appear on earth, in the form of a baby among the Jew. These three teachers were looking for the "Light of Life" for many weeks and when they were about to return to Ur when Zacharias met them and disclosed his belief that Jesus was the object of their quest he sent them to Bethlehem where they found the baby and left their gift with Mary. The baby was almost three weeks old when they visited him. At this juncture, I would like to quote what *The Urantia Book* had to say about this legend.

"Wise men saw no stars to guide them to Bethlehem; the beautiful legend of the star of Bethlehem originated in this way: Jesus was born August 21, at noon 7 B.C. On May 29, 7 B.C., there occurred an extraordinary conjunction of Jupiter and Saturn in the constellation of Pisces. And it is a remarkable astronomic fact that similar conjunctions occurred on September 29 and December 5 of the same year. Upon the basis of these extraordinary, but wholly natural events, the well meaning zealots of the succeeding generation constructed the appealing legends of the star of Bethlehem, and the adoring Magi led to the manger where they beheld and worshiped the new born babe. Oriental and near-Oriental minds delight in fairy stories, and they are continually spinning such beautiful myths about the lives of their religious leaders and political heroes. In the absence of printing, when most human knowledge was passed by word of mouth from one generation to another, it was very easy for myths to become traditions and for traditions to become accepted fact."[6]

Today we need to very seriously reexamine those traditions we accept, that were at one time nothing more than myths. Our ancestors had been conditioned by the early church fathers to accept those myths as facts; they have greatly retarded our spiritual understanding.

The Presentation in the Temple

It was the teaching of Moses that every first born son belonged to the Lord. This son might live if his parents would redeem him by the payment of five shekels to any authorized priest. There was also a Mosaic law which states that a mother after giving birth to a child after a certain period of time has to present herself for purification. It was the custom to perform these two ceremonies at the same time. So Joseph and Mary went to the temple in Jerusalem at the same time to present Jesus to the priest as required for his redemption, and to make the proper sacrifice for Mary's so called purification of the uncleanness of child birth. First they have it in their Laws to be fruitful and multiply, so who was it that decided it was unclean to have a child?

In the courts at Jerusalem temple, lingered two unforgettable characters: Simeon, a singer and Anna, a poetess. Simeon was from Judea and Anna was a Galilean. These two were constantly in each other's company, and both were intimate friends of the priest Zacharias who had revealed the secret of Jesus and John to them. Simeon and Anna yearned for the coming of the Messiah and their respect for Zacharias led them to believe that Jesus was the expected deliverer of the Jewish people. Zacharias knew the day Jesus's parents were scheduled to be at the temple in Jerusalem and he prearranged with Simeon and Anna to let them know by the salute of his up-raised hand which one in the precession of first-born son children was Jesus.

For the occasion, Anna wrote a poem that Simeon agreed to sing. Mary and Joseph were astonished as well as all who were assembled in the temple courts. This was their hymn of the redemption of the first-born sons:

"Blessed be the Lord the God of Israel
For the Lord have visited us and wrought redemption to
his people;

He has raised up a horn of salvation for all of us in the
house of his servant David
Even as he spoke in the mouth of his holy prophets,
Salvation from our enemies and from the hands of all
that hate us;
To show mercy to our fathers, and remember his holy
covenant-
The oath which he swore to Abraham our father,
To grant us that we, being delivered out of the hands of
our enemies,
To serve him without fear,
In holiness and righteousness before him all of our
days,
Yes, you child of promise shall be called the prophet of
the Most High;
For you shall go before the face of the Lord to establish
his kingdom,
To give knowledge of salvation to his people,
In the remission of sin,
Rejoice in the tender mercy of our God because the
dayspring from on high has now visited us.
To shine upon those who sit in darkness and the sha-
dow of death;
To guide our foot into the ways of peace,
And now let your servant depart in peace O Lord ac-
cording to your word,
For my eyes have seen your salvation,
Which you have prepared before the face of all people;
A light for even unveiling the gentiles
And the glory of your people Israel."[7]

On their way back from Bethlehem, Joseph and Mary were silent, confused and awe-struck: Mary was very disturbed by the farewell presentation of Anna, the aged poetess, and, Joseph, leery with the premature effort to make Jesus out of the expected Messiah for the Jewish people.

Herod Acts

It appeared that when the three wise men returned for this ceremony, the spies of Herod were very active; they reported the visit of the priests of Ur to Bethlehem. Herod summoned these Chaldeans to appear before him. He questioned these wise men thoroughly concerning the new "king of the Jews," but they gave him little information explaining that the babe had been born of a woman who had come to Bethlehem with her husband for the census enrollment. But Herod was not satisfied with their answers, he tried to bribe the three wise men by giving them money telling them to find the child and let him know his whereabouts that he may go and worship him also since his kingdom is to be a spiritual kingdom and not a temporal one. When the three wise men did not return, Herod grew suspicious. As he thought these things over in his mind, his spies returned and gave him a full report of what had occurred at the temple in Jerusalem. They even brought him a portion of the song Simeon sung at the redemption ceremonies of Jesus. Herod was extremely angry when the informers failed to follow Mary and Joseph to see which way they were taking the baby. He then sent forth his men to search for the couple and their child. Knowing Herod was pursuing the Nazareth family, Zacharias and Elizabeth stayed away from Bethlehem. The baby Jesus was hidden with Joseph's relatives. Joseph was afraid to look for work, and their small savings was slowly disappearing.

According to *The Urantia Book,* after a little over a year of searching, Herod spies had not found Jesus because Herod and his spies suspected that the baby was still in Bethlehem. Herod gave orders directing a house to house search of every house in Bethlehem, and that every boy baby under two years old should be killed. He was trying to make sure that the child that was to become "King of the Jews" would be destroyed. In one day, sixteen baby boys were slaughtered in Bethlehem of Judea. But intrigue and murder was a common occurrence in the court of Herod, even among his immediate family.

The massacre of these infants took place around the middle of October B.C. 6, when Jesus was a little over a year old. There were believers in the coming Messiah among Herod's political staff, and one of these upon learning of the orders to massacre the baby boys, gave this information to Zacharias, who in turn sent a messenger to Mary and Joseph; and the night before the massacre, Joseph and Mary left Bethlehem with their baby for Alexandria in Egypt. To avoid attracting attention, they traveled alone to Egypt with Jesus. Zacharias provided the money for their trip. In Egypt, Joseph worked at his trade while Mary and Jesus lodged at a well-to-do relative's of Joseph family. They stayed in Alexandria two full years, not returning to Bethlehem until after Herod's death.

The Early Years of Jesus

Due to the anxieties and uncertainties of their stay in Bethlehem, Mary did not wean her baby until they safely arrived in Alexandria, where the family was able to settle down to a normal life. Joseph was well able to care for his family; he found work right after their arrival in Egypt. He was employed as a carpenter for several months, and then he was promoted to foreman of a large group of men working on a public building being constructed at that time. This was a new experience for Joseph, which gave him the idea to become a contractor and builder after their return to Nazareth.

Throughout Jesus' helpless infancy, Mary kept a constant, watchful eye on him. She didn't want anything to happen to her child that would jeopardize his well being or interfere with his mission on earth; no mother was more devoted to her child. In the home where Jesus lived, there lived two other children about his age and among the neighbor there were six other children that were acceptable play-mates. At first, Mary felt she needed to keep Jesus by her side to protect him; she felt something would happen if he was allowed to play in the yard with other children, but Joseph, with the assistance of his kinfolk was able to convince her that it would have a negative effect on his normal growth as a child. It would deprive him of experiences in learning how to adjust himself with children his own age. Mary realized that such protection may cause him to be self-conscious and perhaps self-centered, so she finally gave in and allowed the child of promise to have a normal relationship with other children. But while she was obedient to this decision, she made it her business to always keep a watchful eye on him. Only an affectionate mother could know the burden that she felt in her heart for the safety of her child during the years of his infancy and early childhood.

During their entire stay in Alexandria, which was two years, Jesus enjoyed good health and continued to grow as a normal child. Besides a few friends and relatives, no one was told that Jesus was the "promise child." One of Joseph's relatives revealed this secret to a few friends in Memphis, descendants of Iknaton, and with a small group of Alexandrian believers, gathered at the home of Joseph's relatives, a short time before the couple was to return to Palestine with their "promise child," to wish them farewell. On this occasion, the group that had gathered presented Jesus with a complete Greek translation of the Hebrew Scriptures. The copy of the Jewish sacred writing was not placed in Joseph's hands until both parents had declined the offer of their Alexandrian friend's invitation to remain in Egypt. It was their friends' belief that the child of destiny would have a greater influence on the world from Egypt then any place in Palestine. This attempt to keep Joseph and Mary in Egypt delayed their departure for Palestine, for sometime after they heard the news of Herod's death.

Finally, Mary and Joseph left Alexandria on a boat belonging to their friend named Ezra Eon, headed for Joppa; reaching that port in August B.C. 4, they went to Bethlehem where they spent the entire month of September; there, they were debating with relatives and friends whether to stay there or return to Nazareth. Mary had never really given up the idea that Jesus should be raised in Bethlehem, the City of David. Joseph did not really believe that their son would become a kingly deliverer of Israel. He knew that he was not a descendant of David; that he was recognized among the offspring of David was due to the adoption of one of his ancestors into the Davidic line of descendants. By the first of October Joseph had convinced Mary and their friend that he thought it would be best for the child if they returned to Nazareth. So, early in October B.C. 4, they left Bethlehem for Nazareth, starting early one Sunday morning, Mary and the child riding on their newly acquired beast of burden and Joseph and five relatives proceeded on foot Joseph's relatives had refused to allow them to go alone on the trip to Nazareth.

Back in Nazareth

On the fourth day of the trip, the group reached Nazareth in safety. They arrived unannounced at their home in Nazareth, which had been occupied by Joseph's married brother for more than three years. He was indeed surprised to see them; they had gone so quietly about their business that neither Joseph's family nor Mary's were aware they had ever left Alexandria. The very next day, Joseph's brother moved his family, away and Mary, for the first time since her child was born, settled down with her own little family to enjoy life in their own home. It was less than a week that Joseph found work in his own field as a carpenter. The little family was elated.

Jesus was about three years and two months when they returned to Nazareth. He was in excellent health considering all the traveling he had experienced and was full of childish excitement. Having his own place to run around in and play, he truly missed His playmates in Alexandria, but soon made new friends.

On their way home to Nazareth, Joseph got Mary to agree that it would not be wise to spread the word to their friend and relatives that Jesus was the promised child. They agreed not to mention this matter to anyone, and they both were very faithful in keeping this promise.

Jesus' growth was of normal physical development and the usual activity of a child. He had formed a very close relationship with a neighborhood boy about his age named Jacob. Jesus and Jacob were always happy in their play, and they grew up to be great friends and loyal companions.

The next important event in the life of this family was the birth of the second child; Jesus was excited to have a baby brother named James, born in the early morning of April 2, B.C. 3, and Jesus would stand around by the hour to observe his baby brother's early activities just as most children would do. In midsummer of the same year, Joseph built a small carpentry shop close to the village spring and near a lot where the caravan stayed as they traveled back and forth. After this, Joseph did very little carpentry work during the day. He had two of his brothers working with him and several other mechanics, who he sent out to work, while he remained at the shop making yokes and plows and other woodwork. The Urantia Book states, when Jesus was not in school, he spent an equal amount of time helping his mother at home and at his father's carpentry shop. He was watching the work being done in the shop and listening to the conversations and gossip of the caravan conductors and passengers from around the world. In July of that year, a month before Jesus turned four, an outbreak of malignant intestinal troubles spread all over Nazareth from contact with the caravan travelers. Mary became so frighten that her children might be exposed to the disease that she wrapped both her children and fled to her brother's country home several miles south of Nazareth near the Megiddo road close to Sarid. They did not return to their home for more than two months; Jesus really enjoyed this as it was his first time on a farm.

In a little more than a year after they returned to Nazareth the boy Jesus reached the age where he was able to make his first personal and moral decision; and there came to abide with him a Thought Adjuster (the God within), a divine gift from the Paradise Father. This event occurred on February 11, B.C. 2.

I wrote an entire chapter on the God within in my previous book *Journey to Life.* When we reach a certain age and are able to make our first decision, a Thought Adjuster will come and dwell within (the Father within). Jesus was no more aware of the coming of the Divine Adjuster than are the millions upon millions of other children who, before and since that day, have received Thought Adjuster to indwell their minds and work for the ultimate spiritualization of these minds. In the *Bible* 1 Corinthians 3:16, it states: *"Know ye not that ye are the temple of God, and that the spirit of God dwelleth in you."* Jesus was five years old August of that year, about a month before his fifth birthday anniversary in 2 B.C. He was made very happy by the birth of his sister, Miriam, who was born on the night of July 11. During the evening of that next day, Jesus had a talk with his father concerning the birth of different being into the world as separate individuals. The most essential part of Jesus' early education from his parents was in answering his searching and thoughtful inquiries. Joseph never failed in doing his duty in answering Jesus' many questions. From the time Jesus was five years old until he was ten, he was nothing but a walking question mark. Mary and Joseph tried to answer all of his questions, and when they couldn't, they tried to find a satisfactory solution to the problems his alert mind was pondering.

Since returning to Nazareth, Mary and Joseph was very busy rebuilding their home and especially with Joseph building a new carpenter's shop. He was so occupied he had no time to build a crib for James, but this was corrected long before Miriam was born. She had a very comfortable crib to lie in while the family admired her; Jesus was part of all these natural and normal home experience. He sincerely enjoyed his little brother and sister and was a great help to his mother in their care. It was the custom of the Galilean Jews for the mother to take on the responsibility of the training of the child until their fifth birthday, and if the child was a boy, it was then the father duty to take on the responsibility for the Childs education.

Although Joseph took direct responsibility for Jesus' intellectual and religious education, his mother still interested herself in his home training. She taught him to recognize and care for the vines and flowers that grew around the garden and the garden walls, which surrounded the home plot. She also had on the roof of the house (the summer bedroom) shallow boxes of sand in which Jesus drew out maps and did much of his early practice at writing Aramaic, Greek, and later Hebrew; in time, he learned to write and read all three languages.

Jesus appeared to be a perfect healthy child who continued to make normal progress mentally and emotionally. He did experience a mild digestive upset, in the latter part of his fifth year, which was minor. Though Joseph and Mary talked about the future of their oldest child, if we were there, we would only have seen the growing up of a normal, healthy, carefree child, but an extremely inquisitive child of that time. Today, some people believe that Jesus carved birds out of wood during his childhood, then brought them to life.

First, this would have gone against the laws of nature, and surely he would not have done anything like that. Jesus lived the life of a normal child.

With the help of his mother, at six years old, Jesus had mastered the Galilean dialect of the Aramaic language and his father began to teach him Greek. Joseph spoke Aramaic and Greek fluently. The textbook for the study of the Greek language was the Hebrew scripture, a complete version of the laws of the prophets which included the psalm that was a present to Mary and Joseph when they left Egypt. There were only two complete copies of the Hebrew scripture in all of Nazareth and the possession of one of them by the carpenter's family, made their home a much sought after place, which enabled Jesus to meet an almost endless procession of sincere students seeking the truth of life. Before this year ended, Jesus had assumed custody of the priceless manuscript. He was told on his six birthday that the sacred book was given as a gift by Alexandrian friends and relatives. And in a short time he could read it clearly. The boy Jesus encountered his first shock when he was not yet six years old. It was the young child's belief that the two of his parents knew every thing there was to know. Imagine his surprise when he asked his father the cause of a mild earthquake which had occurred. He was shocked when Joseph said *"my son I really do not know."* When Jesus found out that his earthly parents were not all-wise and all-knowing; he was greatly disappointed.

Joseph thought about telling Jesus those earthquakes were caused by God, but he realized that such an answer would bring on more embarrassing questions. Even at an early age, it was very difficult to answer Jesus' questions about physical or social phenomena. That would have been in harmony with the prevailing belief of the Jewish people of that time. But he did not.

Jesus was willing to accept the fact that there was good and evil spirits as the possible explanation of mental and spiritual phenomena, but at an early age, he was doubtful that such unseen forces were responsible for the physical happenings of the natural world.

A little before Jesus was six years old, in the early summer of B.C. 1, Zacharia, Elizabeth, and their son John came to visit Joseph and his family. Jesus and John had a good time during this visit, their first within their memories. The visitors only stayed a few days; the parents talked about many things; they also talked about the future plans of their sons. While the parents were engaged in their discussions, the two young boys played with blocks in the sand on top of the roof and in other ways they enjoyed each other's company. After meeting John, Jesus developed an unusual interest in the history of Israel and asked his father in great details the meaning of the Sabbath rites, the synagogue sermons and the recurring feast commemoration. His father explained the meaning of these things to him.

This was the year that Joseph and Mary had trouble with Jesus about his prayers, as he insisted upon talking to his heavenly Father just about the same way he would his earthly father. He had departed from the more solemn and reverent way of communication with the heavenly Father, and his parents were somewhat up set, especially his mother. But there was no persuading him to change; he would say his prayers just as he had been taught. Afterward, he was determined to have "just a little talk with his Father in heaven."

In June of the same year Jesus turned six, Joseph turned his shop over to his brothers and formally entered his work as a builder. Before the year was out, their family income had more than tripled. They never again saw the eyes of poverty until after Joseph's death. The family grew larger and larger, and they spent a great deal of money on extra education. They also did quite a bid of traveling, but Joseph's increasing income kept pace with the spending. For the next few years, Joseph had plenty of work at Cona,

The Real Jesus

Bethlehem (of Galilee), Magdala, Nain, Sepphoris, Capernaum and Endor. He also had plenty of work at Nazareth. When James reached the age that he was able to help his mother around the house with the younger children, Jesus spent more time with his father away from home on trips to those surrounding towns and villages. Jesus' teacher acumen helped him to gain a great deal of knowledge from these trips away from home; he was constantly storing knowledge regarding man and the way he lived on earth.

This was the year that Jesus made great progress in the control of his feelings and powerful impulses to the command of family co-operation and discipline at home. Mary was a loving mother, but she was also a strict disciplinarian. In ways Joseph appeared to have had the greater control over Jesus; it was his practice to sit down with Jesus and really explain the necessity of disciplinary curtailment of our personal desire for the betterment of the family as a whole. When the situation was explained to him, he was a more willing participant in doing the wishes of his parents and co-operation with family regulation. In his spare time when, his mother did not need him, Jesus studied the flowers and plants by day and the stars at night.

The Seventh Year A.D. 1

The play life of the Jewish children was rather confined; too often, the children played at the more serious things they saw their parents doing. They played wedding games, pretending someone was getting married, or pretended there was a funeral, which they frequently saw and was so spectacular to them. They danced and sang, and they had only a few organized games, in comparing to the games later children enjoyed. Jesus along with a neighbor's boy and later his brother James enjoyed playing in the far corner of the family carpentry shop where they had fun shaving wood and playing with blocks of wood. Although it was difficult for Jesus to understand the harm in certain kinds of play which was forbidden on the Sabbath, he never failed to obey his parents' wishes. He had a great sense of humor at play, but had little opportunity to express it in the environment of his day and generation. In his seventh year Jesus was cheerful and lighthearted most of the time.

Jesus' mother maintained a cote for doves, which she kept on top of the animal house adjoining their home, and they used the profits of the sale of doves for a special charity fund, which Jesus took care of after he deducted the tithe and turned it over to one of the officers of the synagogue.

Up to this time, the only real accident Jesus had been in was a fall down the back-yard stone stairs that led up to the canvas-roofed bedroom. It happened during an unexpected July sandstorm from the east. The hot winds were carrying a blast of fine sand which usually blew during the rainy season, mostly in March and April. It was unusual to have a storm of this nature in July. When the storm came up, Jesus was on the rooftop playing, which he usually did during the dry season. He was blind by the sand and fell while trying to descend the stairs. After that accident, Joseph built balusters on both sides of stairway. But this accident could not have been avoided; it was not charged to the midwayer and guardian seraphim as negligence that was responsible for the overlooking of Jesus. All of us have guardian angels watching over us to some extent, but we can understand that they were much more concerned in Jesus' case. When this accident occurred, Joseph was away in Endor, and it caused an overdevelopment of anxiety to overtake Mary's mind so much so that she unwisely tried to keep Jesus by her side for months.

After this paragraph, the midwayer that was responsible for these papers made a statement, which I would like to quote at this time.

"*Material accident common place occurrences of a physical nature are not arbitrarily interfered with by celestial personalities under ordinary circumstances. Only midway creatures can intervene in the material condition to safeguard the persons of men or women of destiny, and even in special situations, these being can so act only in obedience to specific mandates of their superiors.* " [8]

This was only one of the minor accidents that Jesus experienced during his inquisitive and adventurous youth. If you can imagine the childhood of an aggressive young boy, then you'll have an idea of the youth life of Jesus and would be able to envisage just about how much anxiety he caused his parents, especially his mother.

Chapter 2

The School Days

When Jesus reached seven years old, the age Jewish children begin their formal education in the synagogue school he started school, in Nazareth. At the time Jesus entered school, he already knew how to read, write, and speak two different languages fluently: Aramaic and Greek. He was now ready to learn to read, write and speak the Hebrew language. He was ready for the task.

From age seven to ten, Jesus attended the elementary school of the Nazareth synagogue. There, he studied the basics of the Book of the Law as it was written in the Hebrew tongue. The next three years, he studied in the advanced school and committed to memory by rote, practicing aloud the Book of the Law. Jesus graduated from the synagogue during his thirteenth year and was turned over to his parents by the over-lookers of the synagogue as an educated "son of the commandments." Jesus was now considered a responsible citizen of the nation of Israel and this entitled him the right to attend his first Passover that year with his mother and father.

The students at the school of Nazareth sat on the floor in a semicircle while their teacher, the chazan, or officer of the synagogue, sat facing them. They begin their studies with the book of "Leviticus," and they continued on to the prophets and the psalms. In the summer months, the hours they stayed in school was greatly shortened.

Jesus soon became a master of the Hebrew language and when there was no one of importance passing through Nazareth, he was often asked to read the Hebrew Scriptures

50

to those that were assembled at the synagogue for the regular Sabbath service.

As I searched through the seven hundred pages or more in *The Urantia Book*, on Jesus I was astounded at the details the midwayer presented on the life and teachings of Jesus. He also touched upon the character of the Apostles that the world's greatest psychiatrists would have trouble trying to do a better job.

To add to his formal schooling, Jesus began to experience the contacting of human nature through people from the four quarters of the world as men from many lands passed through his father's shop. When he grew older, he interacted with the caravan's travelers as they gathered near the spring to rest and for nourishments. Jesus, being able to speak Greek fluently, had no problem conversing with most of the caravan's travelers or their leaders.

In the latter part of June of the year A.D. 3, Jesus along with his father, climbed to the apex of Mount Tabor. It was a nice, clear day and the view was excellent. It seemed to this nine-year old boy that he had really gazed upon the whole world except India, Africa, and Rome.

Jesus' second sister, Martha was born on a Thursday night September 13, A.D. 3, three weeks after the birth of Martha, Joseph was home for awhile. He had started to build an extra room to the house which was a workshop and a bedroom, a small workbench was built for Jesus, and for the first time, he had tools of his own. For many years, Jesus worked at his bench and became an expert at building yokes. This winter and the winter following, was the coldest in Nazareth in many years. Jesus was familiar with seeing snow on the mountains and there were times that it snowed in Nazareth staying on the ground for only a short time; but it was not until this winter did he see ice. The fact that water could be in three different states a—solid, liquid, and a— vapor caused him to ponder for a long time. This caused Jesus to think about the physical world and its constitution.

The personality embodied in this growing youth was all the while the actual creator and organizer of all these things throughout the far-flung universe, but at that age, he didn't have a clue. In fact, Jesus lived a normal human life until he was thirty-one and one-half years old. It wasn't until He was baptized by John the Baptist, did He realize his full divinity.

At ten years old, around the fifth of July of the year A.D. 4, while strolling through the countryside with his father, Jesus gave an indication that he was becoming self-conscious of the unusual nature and purpose of being on earth. Joseph listened admirably and attentively at his son, but did not volunteer any information. The next day Jesus had a talk with his mother on the same subject concerning the increasing revelation within his own consciousness regarding the nature of his personality and his mission on earth. Mary did as Joseph, listened, but gave no information; they thought it best for him to find out through his own experience.

That August A.D. 4, he entered the advance school of the synagogue; he was constantly getting into trouble because of the persistent questions he would ask. His parents were reluctant to stop him from asking these disturbing questions, but his main teacher was greatly fascinated by Jesus' curiosity, insight and hunger for knowledge.

Jesus' playmates saw nothing supernatural in the way he acted because in most ways, he was like them. His interest in learning was somewhat above average, but not unusual. He did ask more questions in school than most. Perhaps the most unusual thing about Jesus was his unwillingness to fight for his rights. He was a developed boy for his age, but it seemed strange to his playmates that he wasn't interested in defending himself, even if subjected to personal abuse. Although he did not suffer much because of this trait, that was due to his friendship with a neighborhood boy who was one year older than Jesus. He was the son of a stone mason, a business associate of Joseph. Jacob admired Jesus, and he made sure that no one picked on him because of his dislike for physical combat. Several older crude boys tried to bully Jesus several times knowing his reputation for docility; they suffered swift retribution from his ever-ready friend Jacob, the mason's son.

This year, Jesus began to show a preference for associating with older persons he liked talking to them about cultural, education, social, political and religious matters. His depth of reasoning and keenness of mind, and his charm delighted the older people; they always enjoyed talking with him. Later that year, Jesus went on a fishing trip with his uncle for two months on the Sea of Galilee. Before he attained manhood, he had become an expert fisherman. His physical development was great. He was an advanced, privileged student at school. He got along well with his younger brothers and sisters at home, having the advantage of being three and one-half years older than the oldest one. He was liked in Nazareth, except for the parents of some of the more troublesome children who thought Jesus impudent. He was a natural teacher as it was difficult for him to refrain from trying to teach and engage in play. Joseph taught Jesus early the diverse ways of making a living explaining the advantage of agriculture over industry and trade. On his first trip with his father to the fishing industry on Lake Galilee, Jesus liked it so much that he just about made up his mind to become a fisherman as a means of making a living. But working at his father's vocation as he grew older enticed him to become a carpenter, and later, a combination of different influences led him to his final choice to become a spiritual leader of a new order. As I mentioned before, Jesus had a normal childhood. He had good, caring parents, but at fourteen and fifteen, things changed drastically for him; as the old saying goes "all hell broke loose."

On Wednesday evening, June 24, A.D. 5, Jude was born. Mary had complications with this birth, the seventh child. She was very ill for several weeks. Joseph had to stay home. Jesus was very busy running errands for his father and with many other duties that he had to do, due to his mother's illness. From this time on this youth was never able to return to his childlike situation of earlier years. From the time of his mother's sickness, Jesus was forced to take on the responsibilities of the first-born son. But he took these burdens on two years before they normally would have fallen on his shoulders.

Jesus' chazan or teacher spent one evening a week with him helping him to master the Hebrew Scriptures. This chazan was very interested in the progress of his intelligent student and he was willing to help in any way he could. This Jewish teacher was a great influence upon the growing mind of Jesus. He, never understood why Jesus showed no interest when he suggested the prospect of Jesus going to Jerusalem to continue his education under the rabbis. In the middle of May of that year, Jesus went on a business trip with his father to Scythopolis, the chief Greek city of Decapolis, the ancient Hebrew Beth-Shean. As they walked about leisurely, Joseph reminisced about the history of his people the story of Saul, the Philistines and Israel trouble history. Jesus was extremely impressed by the cleanliness and well kept arrangement of this so called "heathen" city. He was excited at seeing the open-air theater and was amazed at the beautiful marble temple dedicated to the worship of the "heathen" gods. Joseph was very disturbed by his excitement and tried to counteract this favorable impression by telling him of the beauty and grandeur of the Jewish temple at Jerusalem. Jesus had often gazed upon this magnificent Greek city from the hills of Nazareth and often asked his father about this Greek city, but Joseph always avoided answering those questions. Now they were face to face with these beautiful gentiles city. Joseph could no longer ignore Jesus' question.

At the same time that Joseph and Jesus visited Scythopolis, they had their annual competitive games and public demonstration of physical power between the Greek cities of

The Real Jesus

Decapolis in progress at the Scythopolis amphitheater. Joseph didn't want to go and see the games; the Jews thought the games were all about the "heathen" vain-gloriousness, but Jesus insisted that his father take him to see the games. After the games were finished, Joseph received the surprise of his life. Jesus approved of the games, and suggested that it would be a good idea for the young men of Nazareth to engage in wholesome outdoor physical activities. Joseph talked to Jesus for a long time about the evil nature of such practices, but he knew that Jesus was unconvinced.

That night in their room in the inn, during the course of their discussion, Jesus forgot the trends of the Jewish thoughts and suggested that they go back home and work toward the building of an amphitheater at Nazareth. When Joseph heard his first born-son express such anti-Jewish sentiments, he lost his cool; he snatched Jesus by the shoulder and angrily said, *"My son, never again let me hear you give utterance to such evil thoughts as long as you live."* Jesus was surprised at his father's sudden display of emotion; never before was he made to feel the personal effect of his father's righteous indignation. Jesus was astonished, shocked beyond expression. His only reply was "Very well, my father, it shall be so."

Jesus never again mentioned or alluded to the games or other activities of the Greeks as long as his father lived. Sometimes after that, Jesus saw the Greek's amphitheater at Jerusalem and learned how much the Jews deplored such activities. All through Jesus' life, he tried to introduce the idea of wholesome play and recreation into his personal life and as far as the Jewish practice would allow, into the activities of his twelve apostles.

By the end of Jesus' eleventh year, he was a well developed, somewhat humorous and fairly lighthearted youth. But from this year on, he was more given to periods of profound meditation and serious reflection. He thought about how he could fulfill his obligation to his family and at the

The Twelfth Year (A.D. 6)

This year was eventful for Jesus; he continued to make progress in school and was very diligent in his studies of nature. He began to perform regular work in the home carpentry shop and permitted to manage his own earnings. This year he also learned to keep special matters a secret in the family. He was becoming aware of the way he caused trouble in the village, and was becoming a little more discreet in concealing things that would cause him to be different from his fellow peers. All through this year, he experienced much doubt and uncertainty regarding the nature of his mission. His naturally developing human mind did not yet fully grasp the reality of his dual nature. From this point on, he was able to get along with his brothers and sisters more successfully. He was tactful and compassionate. He thought about their welfare and he enjoyed a good relationship with them. But this was a trying time for Mary and Joseph to take on the rearing of this unprecedented combination of divinity and humanity.

At this stage, Jesus had reached the age of young manhood. He formally graduated from the synagogue school that qualified him to participate in the celebration of his first Passover. The Passover feast this year was on a Saturday, April 9, A.D. 7. That Monday, April 4, a significant amount of people, 103, were traveling from Nazareth to Jerusalem. They traveled south toward Mount Gilboa into the Jordan Valley. They wanted to avoid going through Samaria. Joseph and his family would have enjoyed the trip going through Samaria, going by Jacob's well on by Bethel. The Jewish people dislike dealing with the Samaritans, so Joseph and his family decided to go along with the group by way of the Jordan Valley.

It had been many years since Herod died. Twelve years had also passed since the first Herod tried to destroy the babe of Bethlehem, and no one thought of connecting that affair with this obscure lad of Nazareth.

They went through several historical cities before reaching Jerusalem, and Joseph related the story of each of these historical places to Jesus. Soon, they reached the place they had prearranged to stay during the Passover week, a home of a well-to-do relative of Mary's, one who knew of the early history of John and Jesus through Zacharias. The following day of preparation, they got ready for the appropriate celebration of the Passover Sabbath.

The day before the Passover Sabbath, Jesus' mortal mind was flooded with spiritual illumination and his heart was overcome with compassionate pity for those spiritually blind and the morally ignorant multitudes that gathered for the celebration of the Passover. This was one of the most commemorative days the Son of God spent in the flesh; that night, for the first time in his life on earth, there appeared a messenger from Salvington (the headquarters of the local universe) that was sent by Immanuel who said, *"The hour has come. It is time that you begin to be about your Father's business" The Urantia Book*.

The midwayer that presented these papers admitted that as time passed, the mystery of the incarnation of Jesus became so unfathomable they could hardly understand that this lad of Nazareth was the creator of all Nebadon (the local universe), nor did they understand how the spirit of the same Creator Son, and the spirit of his Paradise Father, was connected with the soul of mankind. They said with the passing of time they were able to see that Jesus' mind was increasingly discerning while he lived his life in the flesh, but in spirit, on his shoulder rested the responsibility of the universe.

At this point, the midwayer said that the career of the Nazareth boy was over, and began the narrative of that adolescent youth. The increasingly self-conscious, divine human now began to ponder His world career. He endeavored to understand his expanding life purpose and the desires of his parents, his obligation to his family and society of his times.

Jesus at Jerusalem

No experience in all of Jesus' eventful life was more exciting and more humanly thrilling than his first remembered visit to Jerusalem. He was especially excited about his experience of attending the temple in discussion, all by himself, which long stood out in his memory as the great event of his later childhood and early youth. This was Jesus' first opportunity to enjoy a few days of independent living, the excitement of being able to come and go without restriction.

Women seldom went to the Passover feast. The men claimed it was not necessary for them to be there. But Jesus refused to go unless his mother went along with them. When Jesus' mother decided to go, many other women wanted to make the trip. That Passover had the largest number of women in proportion to men ever to go up to the Passover from Nazareth.

From leaving home, until they reached the summit of Mount Olives, Jesus was experiencing anxiety of expectation and anticipation. Throughout his childhood, he had heard people talk reverently about Jerusalem and its temple; now he was going to see it with his own eyes. Gazing upon the temple from the height of Mount Olive and from the outside as he got closer to the temple, was all and more than Jesus had expected; but once he entered its sacred portals, he was amazed at what he saw, his disillusionment began.

With his parents by his side, Jesus passed through the temple enclosures between the buildings on his way to join the new sons of the law who were about to be consecrated as citizens of Israel. Jesus was somewhat disappointed by the general demeanor of the temple's great crowd. But the shock of the day came when his mother left them to go to the women's gallery. It never dawned on Jesus that his mother would not be allowed to be with him during the consecrations ceremonies. Jesus was deeply hurt that she had to suffer such unjustly discrimination. He strongly resented this act toward his mother; but other than saying a few words of protest to his father, he said nothing else. But he thought deeply about this as his inquiry to the scribes and teachers a week later would show.

He passed the consecration rituals, but he was very disappointed at its superficial and routine nature. He missed the personal interest which he was so familiar with at the ceremonies of the synagogue at Nazareth. After the ceremonies, he then returned to meet his mother and get ready to go with his father on his first sightseeing tour about the temple and its various courts, galleries and corridors. The temple courts could hold two thousand worshipers at one time; the vastness of the building was mind boggling.

He felt that many of the temple rituals was very touching, beautiful and symbolic, but he was disappointed with the explanation of the real meaning of these ceremonies. Jesus wouldn't accept an explanation of worship or religious devotion, which claimed a belief in the wrath of God or anger of the Almighty. As Jesus and his parents continued to discuss those questions about God after the conclusion of his temple visit, his father became somewhat insistent that he acknowledge the Orthodox Jewish belief. Jesus was so disappointed in his parents that he suddenly turned upon them and looking into his father's eyes said, *"My father it cannot be true, the Father in heaven so regard his erring children on earth. The heavenly Father cannot love his children less than you love me. And I well know, no matter what unwise things I might do, would you never pour out wrath upon me nor vent anger against me. If you my earthly father possess such human reflection of the divine, how much more must the heavenly Father be filled with goodness and overflowing with mercy? I refuse to believe that my Father in heaven loves me less than my father on earth.*"[1]

When Mary and Joseph heard these words of their oldest son, they kept quiet and they never again tried to change his mind about the love of his heavenly Father and the mercifulness of our Father in heaven.

Continuing wherever Jesus went with his father through the temple courts, he was shocked and sickened by the lack of reverence and disrespect. The conduct of the crowd was appalling and they were not consistent with their being in "his Father's house." Jesus also received the shock of his young life when his father took him into the chambers of the gentiles with its consistent noisy chattering and cursing, with the bleating sound of sheep' the overbearing noises of the money changers and the vendors of sacrificial animals, and other commercial commodities. He was also shocked at the spiritual ugliness he saw on the faces of so many of the unthinking worshipers.

They went down to the priests' court beneath a rock ledge in front of the temple, where the altar stood. There, Jesus observed the killing of the doves and other animals, the washing away of blood from the officiating slaughter priest's hands, the horrifying sounds of the dying animals and the blood stained pavement. The horrifying sight sickened the boy from Nazareth. He clutched his father's hands and begged his father to take him away from that terrible place. They went back through the court of the gentiles, and the coarse laughter and cursing was almost a blessing in comparison to sights he had just witnessed. Jesus was horrified at the so called sacrifice to God.

We of today fail to investigate the basis for some of our beliefs; God is responsible for the creation of all things. Why would he need anyone to sacrifice anything to him? This is just an extension of the archaic cave man mentality that created their own gods and tried to please them through unbelievable sacrifices of humans and animals; it has continued to our day with the sacrificial lamb. Jesus never mentioned that he was a sacrificial lamb; even the thought of animals being killed as sacrifice was horrifying to him. What would he think of a human being sacrificed? Here, I want to fast forward Jesus' life a couple of years.

The Two Crucial Years

The midwayer states that of all of Jesus' earthly life experience, the fourteenth and fifteenth years were the most crucial. During these two years, he became somewhat aware of his divinity and destiny. These two years were the most trying for him. It was these two years that should have been called the greatest temptation, the greatest test of his life. No human youth that passed through this stage of confusion and adjustment of problems from adolescence ever experienced a more crucial time than that which Jesus passed through during his transition from childhood to a young man.

As Jesus grew older, his pity and love for the Jewish people deepened. As the years passed, he developed a righteous resentment of the presence in the Father temple of the politically appointed priests. Jesus had great respect for the sincere Pharisees and the honest scribes; he held the hypocritical Pharisees and dishonest theologians in contempt.

When Jesus scrutinized those leaders of Israel, he was tempted to look at the possibility of becoming the Messiah of the Jewish expectations, but he never succumbed to that temptation.

The story of Jesus' daring act among the wise men of the temple of Jerusalem was satisfying to all of Nazareth, especially his formal teachers in the synagogue school. For a while, Jesus' praise was on everyone's lips; the whole village talked about his childhood wisdom and predicted that he was sure to become a great leader of Israel, a great teacher coming out of Nazareth of Galilee. They all looked forward to the day Jesus would turn fifteen so that he'd be permitted to read from the scriptures regularly in the synagogue on the Sabbath day.

Jesus' Fourteenth Year (A.D. 8)

By age fourteen, Jesus became a good yoke maker and worked canvas and leather; he was also developing his skill as an expert carpenter and cabinetmaker. That summer, he often made trips to the top of the hill northwest of Nazareth where he prayed and meditated. He was becoming more aware of the nature of his bestowal on earth.

This hill that he frequently visited a little over one hundred years prior to that was known as the site of Baal. Now it is the place of the tomb of Simeon, a well known holy man of Israel at that time.

"From the summit of this hell of Simeon, Jesus looked out over Nazareth and the surrounding counties. He would gaze upon Megiddo and recall the story of the Egyptian army winning its first great victory in Asia, and how later on, another such army defeated the Judean king, Josiah. Not far away, he could look upon Taanach, where Deborah and Barak defeated Sisera. In the distance, he could view the hills of Dothan, where he had been taught that Joseph's brethren gave him into Egyptian slavery. He then would shift his gaze over to Ebal Gerizim and recount to himself the traditions of Abraham, Jacob and Abimelech. And this he recalled and turned over in his mind the historic and traditional events of his father Joseph's people."[2]

The Real Jesus

Jesus continued with his advanced course of reading the scriptures under the synagogue teacher. He also continued with the education of his sisters and brothers, as they grew to the age where they could be taught. The early part of that year Joseph set aside income from the profit of his Nazareth and Capernaum property to pay for Jesus' additional long course of study at Jerusalem. It was planned that Jesus would go to Jerusalem that August of the following year when he would be fifteen.

By the end of Jesus' fourteenth year, Joseph and Mary had considerable doubts about the destiny of their oldest son. He was a brilliant and lovable son, but was very difficult to understand. The depth of his mind was too hard to fathom, but nothing miraculous ever happened. Many times his mother stood in breathless anticipation expecting something supernatural to happen. Her hopes were destroyed in sad disappointment. The Jews of that time always believed that the prophets and men of promise always demonstrated their calling by performing some kind of miracle and working wonders. But Jesus did none of these things, which greatly confused his parents.

CHAPTER 3

The Death of Joseph

The family of Jesus was doing well until one fatal day Tuesday, September 25 A.D. 8 a runner from Sepphoris brought to this Nazareth home the news that Joseph had been seriously injured by the falling of a derrick while he was working on the governor's residence. The runner from Sepphoris stopped by Joseph's shop on the way to his home to inform Jesus of his father's accident. They went together to Jesus' home to break the news to Mary. Jesus wanted to go right away to his father, but Mary's only thought was that she had to hasten to her husband's side. She wanted James, who was then ten, to go with her while Jesus stayed home with the younger children until she returned. She did not know how seriously Joseph was hurt. But Joseph had died of his wounds before Mary arrived. They brought his body back to Nazareth. The next day, they laid him to rest alongside his father.

Just when everything seems to be going well for this family, the future was looking bright, suddenly; it seemed that a cruel hand struck down the head of this family. All of the affairs of this house were destroyed; all of Jesus' plans for future education were annihilated. This boy carpenter just turned fifteen had a difficult future ahead. He awakened to the realization that not only did he have to fulfill the duty of his heavenly Father, but he also must shoulder the responsibilities of caring for his widowed mother and seven brothers and sisters, and another yet to be born.

Jesus now became the sole supporter and comforter of this suddenly bereaved family. It seemed as though the accident was permitted as the natural order of events and was allowed to take place as far as the young lad of destiny was concerned. Yet, he was so young to assume the heavy burden. Though he was highly educated and disciplined, which he needed to take on the responsibility of becoming the head of the family. This entails the caring for his sisters, brothers, supporting and protecting his mother. Accepting the responsibility that was suddenly thrust upon him, he preformed his duties until the end.

He wasn't expected now to go to Jerusalem and study under the rabbis and he didn't want to; at least one problem that he expected difficulties in his life has been tragically solved, it was truly said that Jesus, "sat at no man's feet." He was willing to learn even from the smallest child. He never received authority to teach truth from human source. Jesus knew nothing about Gabriel, visit to his mother before he was born; he learned about it from John on the day of his baptism at the beginning of his public ministry.

As the years passed Jesus, the young carpenter of Nazareth began to study different institutions of society and how they was used, inquiring what does it do for the human soul? Does it bring God to man? Does it bring man to God? But Jesus did not exactly neglect the recreational or social aspect of life. He devoted most of his energies to two things: the taking care of his family and the preparation for the doing of his heavenly Father's will on earth.

This is the year that it became the habit of the neighbors to drop in during the evening to hear Jesus play the harp, to listen to his stories (Jesus was a great story teller) and to hear him read from the Greek scripture. The economic situation of the family continue to run without problems as there was quite a sum of money that Joseph had left behind. Also Jesus had shown at an early age his abilities to administer his father's estate; he had demonstrated keen business and financial shrewdness.

But in spite of all the efforts of Jesus and his neighbors, they couldn't bring happiness to the home. Mary and the

The Fifteenth Year (A.D. 9)

Here, the midwayer said he was reckoning time in accordance with the twentieth century calendar, not by the Jewish calendar.

Jesus had taken a firm grip on the caring for his family, but their savings was depleting fast. He realized the necessity of selling one of the Nazareth houses that Joseph and his neighbor Jacob had owned in partnership.

On Wednesday evening, April 17, A.D. 9, the eighth child, Ruth, was born, and to the best of his ability, Jesus tried to take the place of his father by comforting the baby and helping his mother at this difficult time. For almost ten years until the beginning of his ministry, Jesus nurtured and cared for his little sister Ruth, and the rest of his brothers and sisters. No father could have cared for them better than Jesus. After his father's death, Jesus tried to teach his older brothers and sisters how to express themselves individually in prayer, as he enjoyed doing, but they could not grasp this thought and returned to their memorized form of praying. It was during this year that Jesus formulated "The Lord's Prayer" which he later taught his apostles. In a way, "The Lord's Prayer" was an evolution to the way the family was use to praying, at their altar they had several forms of prayers.

Jesus gave up on the idea of having each individual formulating their prayer. One evening in the month of October, he sat down by a little squat lamp that was on the low stone table, and on a piece of smooth cedar board and a piece of charcoal he wrote out "The Lord's Prayer" that became the standard family partition. During this time, Jesus was troubled by confused thoughts he knew that family responsibility came first, so he removed thoughts of going to Jerusalem to study. Jesus correctly reasoned that the care of his father family came first since he was the oldest child: that was his obligation.

Sometime during that year, Jesus ran across a statement in *The Book of Enoch* that had a great influence in his adopting the term "Son of Man" as a designation for his bestowal mission on Urantia. He greatly considered the Jewish idea of the Messiah; he knew definitely that he was not to be that Messiah. He longed to help his father's people, but he never desired to lead a Jewish army to overthrow the foreign domination of Palestine. He knew that he would never sit on the throne of David at Jerusalem. Nor did Jesus believe his mission was just for the Jewish people. In no sense could his life mission be the fulfillment of the longings and supposed Messianic prophecies of Hebrew Scriptures, at least not as the Jew understood those prediction of the prophets, and certainly not as the prophet Daniel depicted the "Son of Man."

If we in the Western World paid attention years ago to records like the Sumerian cuneiform, we would have known years ago that many other races of people were expecting a "Son of God" many years before the Jewish people ever thought of becoming a race of people as far back as Adam and Eve over thirty-six thousand years ago.

While Jesus was turning all of these things over in his mind he found in the synagogue in Nazareth a manuscript called *The Book of Enoch,* and he knew that it wasn't written by Enoch of old. Still it was very interesting to him he read and reread it many times.

"There was one passage which particularly impressed him, a passage in which the term "Son of Man" appeared. The writer of this so called Book of Enoch went on to tell about this "Son of Man," describing the work that he would do on earth and explaining that this "Son of Man," before

coming down on this earth to bring salvation to mankind, had walked through the courts of heavenly glory with his Father, the Father of all; and that he turned his back on all this grandeur and glory to come on earth to proclaim salvation to the needy mortal. As Jesus would read passages (well understanding that much of the Eastern Mysticism which had became admixed with these teachings was erroneous), he responded in his heart and recognized in his mind that of all the Messianic prediction of the Hebrew scriptures and all the theories about the Jewish deliverer, none was so near the truth as the story tucked away in this only partially accredited Book of Enoch; and he then and there decided to adopt as his inaugural title "The Son of Man." And this he did when he subsequently began his public work. Jesus had an unerring ability for recognition of truth and truth he never hesitated to embrace no matter from what source it appeared to emanate."[1]

One thing this passage brings out is that Jesus was in his glory with the Father before coming to our earth to bring us salvation not as a sacrificial lamb, but with the truth. He said, "The truth will set you free."

By this time, Jesus had about settled, in his mind his coming work for the world. But he kept this to himself. He didn't tell his mother who still held onto the concept of him becoming the Jewish Messiah. The confusion of Jesus' younger days were somewhat settled now, that he understood something about the nature of his mission on earth: "to be about his Father's business" to show his Father's loving nature to all mankind. He began to rethink the many statements in the scriptures that refer to the coming of a national deliverer, a Jewish teacher or king. He wondered who or what these prophecies referred to. Wasn't he a Jew or was he? Was he from the House of David? His mother believed that he was, but his father that he was not. So he decided that he was not. He also wondered had the prophets confused the nature and mission of the Messiah.

Mary saw how the family funds were disappearing, so she turned the sale of the doves over to James. They bought a second cow and with the help of Miriam, they began to sale milk to their Nazareth neighbors.

According to *The Urantia Book* Jesus' profound period of meditation, his frequent trips to the hilltop to pray and the strange ideas he talked about every now and then, upset his mother; she sometimes thought that Jesus was a little "touched." Then, she would come to her senses remembering that he was a child of promise, and in some ways, different than other children.

Jesus was learning not to speak about everything that came to his mind, not even to his mother. He talked less about those things that the average person couldn't understand, which would lead to his being looked upon as more different than ordinary folks. Jesus longed for someone that would understand his problems. He yearned for a friend that would understand him, but his problems were too complex for his human associates to understand. Therefore the uniqueness of his situation forced him to bear his burden alone.

The Sermon in the Synagogue

Now that he was fifteen, he could lawfully occupy the synagogue pulpit on the Sabbath day. Often in the absence of speakers, Jesus was asked to read the scriptures. Now the time had come when, according to law, he could conduct services. On the first Sabbath after his fifteenth birthday, the chazan arranged for Jesus to conduct the morning service at the synagogue. When all of the faithful in Nazareth assembled, the young man made his selection of the scriptures stood up and began to read: here, Jesus recited a long reading; he started by saying, *"The spirit of the Lord God is upon me. He has sent me to bring good news to the meek, to bind up the brokenhearted, to proclaim liberty to the captives, and set the spirituals prisoners free."* He continued with his reading and when he finished, he sat down. The congregation went to their home in a state of awe over his words that he so graciously read to them. The townspeople had never seen Jesus so magnificently solemn; they had never heard his voice so sincere, nor seen Jesus so manly and decisive, so in command.

That Sabbath after service, Jesus climbed the Nazareth Hill with James, and afterwards when they returned home, he wrote out the Ten Commandments in Greek on two small boards in charcoal. Martha colored and decorated these boards, and for a long time, they hung on the wall over James' workbench.

The Financial Struggle

Jesus and his family had gradually returned to the simple life of earlier years. Their clothes and food became simpler. They had plenty of milk, butter and cheese. They enjoyed the produce of their garden when in season. But with each passing month, their provisions were getting less and less. Their breakfast was very simple; they saved their best food for the evening meal. But among these Jews, lack of wealth did not mean they were inferior. Jesus at this young age, well understood how man lived in his day; he understood life in the home, field and workshop. Jesus of Nazareth's chazan held to the idea that Jesus would become a great teacher, perhaps the successor of the renowned Gamaliel at Jerusalem. But Jesus was somewhat frustrated about his future; things didn't look as bright as it once did. But he didn't let it get him down. He lived day by day doing his job faithfully and saw that his immediate responsibilities were taken care of.

The pay for carpenter's work was slowly dwindling; by the end of the year, when he was fifteen, Jesus could earn, by starting early and working late, only the equivalent of about twenty-five cents a day. By the next year, it was difficult to pay the civil taxes, not to mention the synagogue and temple tax of a half-shekel. During this year, the tax collectors tried to get extra revenue out of Jesus; they even threatened to take his harp. Jesus was afraid that the tax collectors might find out about the Greek scriptures that were given to him as a gift when he was a baby, and that they might confiscate it for taxes, so he presented it to Nazareth's synagogue library as his maturity offering to the Lord.

One of the great shocks of his fifteenth year came when Jesus went over to Sepphoris to receive the decision from Herod in regards to the appeal in a dispute taken to Herod concerning the amount of money due to Joseph at the time of his accidental death. Mary and Jesus expected a considerable sum of money, but the treasurers at Sepphoris offered a trifling sum. Joseph's brother had taken the appeal to Herod himself, Jesus stood in the palace and heard Herod decree that his father had nothing due him at the time of his death. With such an unjust decision, Jesus never trusted Herod Antipas. This is no doubt the reason Jesus referred to Herod as the cunning fox.

The family supply shop was taken over by his uncles, and Jesus worked out of the home shop to be near his mother in case she needed his help in family matters. Around this time, Jesus began sending his brother James to the camel lot to get information about world events; this is the way he kept pace with the news of the day.

As Jesus grew to manhood, he went through all of the conflicts and confusion the average young person passes through. The rigorous experience of supporting his family was a safety measure against Jesus having time for idle meditation or the indulgence in mystic tendencies.

This was also the year Jesus rented a nice piece of land not too far from their home. He divided the land into family plots, each of his brothers and sisters had a garden plot, and they entered into healthy competition in their agricultural goals. In the evening, their older brother spent time with them in their garden during the season of vegetable cultivation. As Jesus worked with his sisters and brothers, he wished many times that they had a farm in the country where they could be free. But that was wishful thinking; they did not find themselves growing up in the country. Instead he was practical; he vigorously attacked his problems just as he found them. He did everything in his power to adjust himself and his family to the realities of their situation and do with what they had as well as try to improve their living condition.

At one time, Jesus entertained the thought that they could collect a considerable amount of money due to his father for the work he had done on Herod's palace; he thought he might get enough to buy a small farm. He really contemplated on moving his family to the county. But when Herod denied them the money due to Joseph, they gave up on the idea of moving to the county. They tried to enjoy much of the experience of the farm life where they were; they now own three cows, four sheep, and a flock of chickens, a donkey, and a dog also the doves.

Over the years, it crossed my mind several times how could God expect us humans to be like the Christ. According to the Christian Church, Jesus was not conceived in the normal way the rest of us were conceived. If Mary was impregnated by a Higher Being, which is impossible according to the laws of nature, that would also give Him super-human genes. They say that Jesus didn't have a human father. In other words, he was conceived in a supernatural way. How could we that had normal parents compete with a being that started off with a supernatural conception? How could God expect us to be as good as a superhuman being? We can very well say that he had a great advantage over us. Things made much more sense when I read the story in *The Urantia Book.* Joseph was Jesus' real earthly father, and he had to experience all that we had to experience and then some; it's just that he incarnated from the heaven world into a human embryo.

The Seventeenth Year (A.D. 11)

During Jesus' seventeenth year, there were considerable disturbances, more so in Jerusalem and in Judea than anywhere else; many were in favor of rebellion against payment of taxes to Rome. Developing among the Jews was a strong nationalist party, known as the Zealots. The Zealots were not like the Pharisees—willing to wait for the coming of a Messiah. They wanted to bring things to a conclusion through a political revolt.

A group of organizers from Jerusalem arrived in Galilee; they were making good advances until they reached Nazareth. When they went to see Jesus, he listened attentively and asked many question, but refused to join the party. His refusing to join had a negative effect on many of the young people of his area, they wouldn't join either. Mary did her utmost to get Jesus to enlist, but he would not budge. She even went as far as to accuse Jesus of disrespect a violation of his pledge made when they returned to Jerusalem: that he would subject to his parents; but in answer to her accusation, he only laid a kind hand upon her shoulder and looking straight into her face said, "My mother how could you?" Mary withdrew her statement. One of Jesus uncles (Mary's brother Simon) joined the Zealots group and became an officer in the Galilean division. For several years, there was unrest between Jesus and his uncle.

Trouble began to stir in Nazareth. Jesus' attitude about the situation caused a division among the Jewish youth in the city. About half of them joined the Nationalist Organization; the others began creating an opposing group of more moderate patriots. They were expecting Jesus to take over leadership. They were baffled when he refused; for an excuse, he gave his heavy family duties, which they all accepted. But a situation arose when a wealthy Jew, named Isaac, a money lender to the gentiles, came forward and offered to support Jesus' family if he laid down his tools and assumed leadership of one of these Nazareth patriotic groups. Jesus was really in a predicament now; I quote the following so that the reader will get a better understanding of Jesus' situation.

"Jesus then scarcely seventeen years old was confronted with one of the most delicate and difficult situations of his early life. Patriotic issuers, especially when complicated by tax-gathering foreign oppressors, are always difficult for spiritual leaders to relate themselves to, and it was doubly in this case since the Jewish religion was involved in all this agitation against Rome.

Jesus' position was made more difficult because his mother and uncle, and even his younger brother James, all urged him to join the nationalist cause. All the better Jews of Nazareth had enlisted, and those young men who had not joined the movement would all enlist the moment Jesus changed his mind. He had but one wise counselor in all Nazareth, his old teacher, the chazan, who counseled him about his reply to the citizens' committee of Nazareth when they came to ask for his answer to the public appeal which had been made. In all Jesus' young life this was the very first time he had consciously resorted to public strategy. Theretofore, always had he depended upon a frank statement of truth to clarify the situation, but now he could not declare the full truth. He could not intimate that he was more than a man; he could not disclose his idea of the mission which awaited his attainment of a riper manhood. Despite these limitations his religious fealty and national loyalty were directly challenged. His family was in turmoil, his youthful friends in division, and the entire Jewish contingent of the town in a hubbub. And to think that he was to blame for it all! And how innocent he had been of all intention to make trouble of any kind, much less a disturbance of this sort.

The Real Jesus

Something had to be done. He must state his position, and this he did bravely and diplomatically to the satisfaction of many, but not all. He adhered to the terms of his original plea, maintaining that his first duty was to his family, that a widowed mother and eight brothers and sisters needed something more than mere money could buy — the physical necessities of life — that they were entitled to a father's watchcare and guidance, and that he could not in clear conscience release himself from the obligation which a cruel accident had thrust upon him. He paid compliment to his mother and eldest brother for being willing to release him but reiterated that loyalty to a dead father forbade his leaving the family no matter how much money was forthcoming for their material support, making his never-to-be-forgotten statement that "money cannot love." In the course of this address Jesus made several veiled references to his "life mission" but explained that, regardless of whether or not it might be inconsistent with the military idea, it, along with everything else in his life, had been given up in order that he might be able to discharge faithfully his obligation to his family. Everyone in Nazareth well knew he was a good father to his family, and this was a matter so near the heart of every noble Jew that Jesus' plea found an appreciative response in the hearts of many of his hearers; and some of those who were not thus minded were disarmed by a speech made by James, which, while not on the program, was delivered at this time. That very day the chazan had rehearsed James in his speech, but that was their secret.[2]"

James said in essence that he was sure Jesus would help to free his people if he, James, were old enough to take responsibility for their family; and if they would consent to allow Jesus to remain with them to be their father and teacher then soon they will not have just one leader from Joseph's family, but five of his sons would grow up and come forth from their bother-father's guidance to serve the nation. And so James brought to a happy ending a very tense and intimidating situation.

The crisis was over at least for now, but that episode was never forgotten in Nazareth. The aggravation continued; never again was Jesus in universal favor with the Jews; the division of opinion was never overcome. This was one of the main reasons why Jesus later on moved to Capernaum. Thereafter, Nazareth continued in their division concerning the Son of Man.

James finished school that year, and started working full-time at the home carpenter shop. He became a good worker with tools he took over making yokes and plows and Jesus began to do more house finishing and expert cabinet work.

That year, Jesus made great progress in the harnessing of his mind. He gradually brought his divine and human nature together and the discipline of his intellect by the force of his own *decision* and with the aid of his indwelling Thought Adjuster (that God within). So far nothing of a supernatural nature had happened in Jesus' life, except the visit of a messenger, dispatched from the higher world, by Immanuel who once appeared to Jesus during the night in Jerusalem.

Rebecca the Daughter of Ezra

Even though Jesus was poor, his social standing in Nazareth was in no way affected. He was one of the most popular young men in Nazareth, and highly regarded by most of the young of that city. Jesus was a splendid, intellectual young man and considering his prestige as a spiritual leader, it was not unusual that Rebecca, the oldest daughter of Ezra, a wealthy merchant trader of Nazareth realized she was slowly falling in love with this son of Joseph. Rebecca told Miriam, Jesus' sister about her affection for her brother, and Miriam confided in her mother.

Mary was really upset, and she wonder if she would now lose her son, the indispensable head of their family? "Would trouble ever cease?" She thought. Mary then paused to ponder what effect would marriage have upon Jesus' future career; it wasn't often, but sometimes she remembered that Jesus was a child of promise.

After talking the matter over with Miriam, Mary decided to make an effort to stop it before Jesus heard about it. They went directly to Rebecca telling her the whole story about Jesus being a Son of Destiny that he was to become a great religious leader, perhaps the Messiah.

Rebecca was thrilled at what they were telling her. She was now more determined than ever to marry Jesus, she figured, she could help in his career as a religious leader. She said that such a man would all the more need a faithful and efficient wife. She felt that Mary's efforts to dissuade her was only natural, the dread of losing the head and sole supporter of her family; she knew that her father would approve of her interest in the carpenter's son, and she was right when she thought that her father would fully compensate Jesus' family for his lose in earnings. When her father agreed to her plans, Rebecca again sought to see Mary and Miriam, but she failed to win their support, so she went directly to Jesus. She did this with the help of her father who invited Jesus to their home to celebrate Rebecca's seventeenth birthday.

Jesus listened to their proposal attentively. First, he listen to the father, and then to Rebecca; he then kindly replied that no amount of money could take the place of his obligation to rear his father's family, to "fulfill the most sacred of all human trusts—loyalty to ones flesh and blood." Rebecca's father was deeply moved by Jesus' words of family devotion and he retired from the pow-wow; his only words to his wife whose name was also Mary, *"we can't have him as a son; he is too noble for us,"* according to *The Urantia Book.*

Then Jesus began to have a serious talk with Rebecca. So far, in his life, Jesus had made little distinction in his dealings with boys and girls, with young men or young women. His mind was too occupied with everyday passing affairs of everyday living, and in his contemplation of his career of doing his Father's will, he didn't have time to seriously think of human love and marriage. But now he was face to face with another human problem that the average human has to confront and make a decision; this goes to show that Jesus was tested on all points, as we all are.

After listening with intensiveness to Rebecca, Jesus sincerely thanked her for her admiration. He said that it would comfort and cheer him all the days of his life. He expressed that he was not free to enter into a relationship with any woman other than brotherly love and pure friendship; he also explained that his supreme duty right then was the rearing of his father's family and until that was accomplished; marriage was not an option for him. He also informed her that if he was a child of destiny he must not get involved in situations of life long duration, until his destiny is manifested.

Of course Rebecca was heartbroken. She begged her father to move from Nazareth, and her father finally consented and moved to Sepphoris. After this experience, when any man asked Rebecca for her hand in marriage, she refused; she devoted her life to Jesus' course and she followed him devotedly through the eventful years of his public service. She was among the other women by the side of Mary, the mother of Jesus, on the tragic afternoon when the Son of Man was hung upon the cross.

When Jesus was twenty two, he sought employment in Sepphoris and found work there. Before he started his new job, he held one of his periodic family conference, and appointed James as acting head of the family. James was now a little past eighteen. Jesus promised James his support and asked co-operation and obedience from each member of the family. From that day forward, James took on the financial responsibilities of the family, and Jesus, making his weekly contributions to his brother, never returned as head of the family.

The Later Adult Life of Jesus

Jesus had fully disconnected himself from the domestic management of his family. He continued to contribute to the finances of his family right up to his baptism.

Jesus now made every effort to detach himself permanently from his Nazareth home. This was not easy for Jesus as he loved his family and this natural affection had been greatly increased by his extraordinary devotion to them; the family had slowly awakened to the fact that Jesus was making ready to leave them, although, he had prepared them for this departure for almost four years they could not help but feel sadness linger in their hearts.

In January A.D.21, Jesus was twenty seven; on a rainy Sunday morning, he took unceremonious leave of his family, telling them he was going to Tiberias, and then to visit other cities around the Sea of Galilee. He spent a week in Tiberias, the new city that soon took Sepphoris' place as the capital of Galilee; he found little to hold his interest there, so he went on to Magdala and Bethsaida to Capernaum. There, he stopped to visit his father's friend Zebedee. Zebedee's sons John, David and James, were fishermen. Jesus and John became very close friends. He admired Jesus' spiritual intellect. Zebedee was a boat builder. Jesus was an expert at both designing and building, and a master at working with wood; Zebedee had long known of the skills of the Nazareth craftsman.

For a long time, Zebedee had been thinking, of how could he improve on the quality of his boats. He talked his plans over with Jesus and invited him to join in on the enterprise; Jesus immediately accepted. He worked with

Zebedee a little more than one year, and during that time, he created a new type of boat. Using advanced techniques and improved methods of steaming boards, Jesus and Zebedee built boats that were of excellent quality they were much safer than the older types. For several years Zebedee had more work than he could handle making those new types of boats. In less than five years, almost all of the boats on the lake had been built at Zebedee's shop at Capernaum. And Jesus was well-known to the Galilean fisher-people as the designer of the new boats.

In March A.D. 22, Jesus left Zebedee and Capernaum; he was twenty-eight years old. He asked for a small sum of money to pay his expenses at Jerusalem. While Jesus worked for Zebedee, had taken only small sums of money and each month he would send the money to his family in Nazareth.

When Jesus left the Zebedee's family, he agreed to stay in Jerusalem until after the Passover, and they all promised to be there for that event. They even arranged to celebrate the Passover supper together. They all felt sad when Jesus left, especially his daughters; Zebedee had four daughters and three sons. Before leaving Capernaum, Jesus had a long talk with his new friend John Zebedee. He told John that he planned on traveling extensively until *"my time shall come"* and asked John to act on his behalf in sending money to his family in Nazareth each month until the funds due him ran out. John made Jesus this promise: *"My teacher, go about your business, do your work in the world; I will act for you in this or any other matter, and I will watch over your family even as I would foster my own mother and care for my own brothers and sisters. I will disburse your funds which my father holds as you have directed and as they may be needed, and if your mother is in need, then will I share my own earnings with her. Go your way in peace. I will act in your stead in all these matters."*[3]

The whole of Jesus' twenty-ninth year he spent finishing up the tour of the Mediterranean World. Throughout the tour of the Roman world, Jesus was known as the scribe from Damascus. This was an eventful period in Jesus' life. On this journey he made many contacts with his fellow human; this journey was also a phase in his life that he never revealed to any member of his family nor to any of the apostles. Jesus lived out his life and left this world without anyone (but Zebedee of Bethsaida) knowing that he made such an involved trip. Some of his friends thought he had gone to Damascus; others thought he had gone to India. His own family believed he was in Alexandria. When Jesus returned to Palestine, he didn't do anything to change his family's thinking that he had left Jerusalem and journeyed to Alexandria. Only Zebedee the Boat-builder knew for sure where he had been.

The Human Jesus

According to the on looking heavenly celestial intelligences, of our local universe, this Mediterranean experience was the most fascinating of all Jesus' earth experiences up to the time of his crucifixion and mortal death. This was the exciting period of his *Personal-ministry* with the soon to come public ministry. This unique experience was fascinating more so because he was still at this time the carpenter of Nazareth, the boat builder of Capernaum, the scribe of Damascus and the Son of Man. He hadn't completely accomplished the mastery of his human mind; though he was still a man among men. During his twenty-ninth year, Jesus reached the apex of his religious and spiritual growth. This experience of growth was a gradual achievement from the moment of the arrival of his thought adjuster at around six years old until the day of completion, when the material mind and the spiritual became one. Jesus obtained this spiritual in completion the day he was baptized in the Jordan River. This is the same experience the *Bible* claimed Enoch had, where the lower-self and high-self became one, and Enoch was seen no more.

On the Way to Rome

Before starting his trip, by what seemed apparent chance, Jesus met a wealthy traveler named Gonod and his son, a young man around seventeen-years old. They were from India and on their way to visit Rome and other places in the Mediterranean; they had arranged to visit Jerusalem during the Passover hoping to find someone they could hire as an interpreter for the father's business and as a tutor for the son. After meeting Jesus, the father insisted Jesus travel with them. Jesus told the father about his family situation, that his father had died some years before in a construction accident, and he had a responsibility to care for his younger brothers, sisters and his mother. Jesus' parents had eight children, with Jesus being the oldest; only one of the boys was old enough to help care for the family and he was quite young. Jesus told the father it would be unfair to leave them for almost two years. The father agreed to pay Jesus one year's salary in advance; Jesus accepted the father's offer.

Touring the Roman world exhausted most of Jesus' twenty-eighth and the entire twenty-ninth year of his life on earth. He and two natives from India—Gonod and his 17 year old son Ganid—left Jerusalem on Sunday morning, April 26, A.D. 22. They made their journey on schedule. Jesus said good-by to the father and the son on the Persian Gulf on the tenth day of December the following year A.D. 23; in their travels, they had visited around thirty-eight cities and counties.

Jesus worked for four months at Damascus and while there, he learned the basics of the language spoken by Gonod and Ganid. He worked most of the time on translations from Greek into one of the languages of India; he was assisted by a native of Gonod's home district.

The Real Jesus

On the Mediterranean trip, Jesus spent about half of each day teaching Ganid and acting as interpreter during Gonod's business conferences and social contacts. The remainder of his time Jesus devoted to making close personal contacts with his fellow humans; he made intimate associations with the mortals of the earth. This was his activity during the year prior to his public ministry.

An Analysis of Jonah

While in Joppa, Jesus met Gadiah, a Philistine who worked as a tanner for a rich merchant named Simon. Gonad's agent in Mesopotamia transacted lots of business with Simon; Gonod and his son wanted to visit him when they reached Caesarea. While they were in Joppa, Jesus and Gadiah became good friends. Gadiah was a seeker and Jesus was a truth giver; he was the truth for that generation on earth.

One evening after Jesus and the young Philistine finished their evening meal, they strolled by the seashore. Gadiah did not know this "scribe of Damascus" was actually versed in the Hebrew tradition when he pointed out to Jesus the ship landing from which it was believed that Jonah had started on his troubled voyage to Tarshish. When he had finished his remarks, he asked Jesus, *Do you think the big fish really swallowed Jonah?"* Jesus, realizing this young man's life was greatly influenced by this tradition and his concentrating upon it, had impressed upon him the absurdity of trying to run away from his responsibility. Jesus made sure he wouldn't say anything that would suddenly destroy the young man's means for practical living; so answering his question, Jesus said:

"My friend, we are all Jonahs with lives to live in accordance with the will of God, and at all times when we seek to escape the present duty of living by running away to far-off enticements, we thereby put ourselves in the immediate

control of those influences which are not directed by the powers of truth and the forces of righteousness. The flight from duty is the sacrifice of truth. The escape from the service of light and life can only result in those distressing conflicts with the difficult whales of selfishness which lead eventually to darkness and death unless such God-forsaking Jonahs shall turn their hearts, even when in the very depths of despair, to seek after God and his goodness. And when such disheartened souls sincerely seek for God—hunger for truth and thirst for righteousness-there is nothing that can hold them in further captivity. No matter into what great depths they may have fallen, when they seek the light with a whole heart, the spirit of the Lord God of heaven will deliver them from their captivity; the evil circumstances of life will spew them out upon the dry land of fresh opportunities for renewed service and wiser living."[4]

From this actual contact with the people, Jesus acquainted himself with the higher material and intellectual of the occident and the Levant; from Gonod and his bright son he learned a great deal about the civilization and culture of India, and China. Gonod was a citizen of India who had made three extensive visits to the empire of China. The young Ganid learned a lot from Jesus on this extensive and intimate trip so much so they developed a great affection for each other, and the young man's father tried many times to persuade Jesus to return with them to India, but he always refused, telling him of the necessity for his returning to his family in Palestine.

As we all know, Jesus told many stories and gave many parables. One afternoon Jesus and Ganid had both enjoyed playing with a very smart shepherd dog; Ganid asked Jesus if the dog had a soul or whether it had a will. Jesus said in response to this question; *"The dog has a mind which can know material man, his master, but cannot know God, who is spirit; therefore, the dog does not possess a spiritual nature and cannot enjoy a spiritual experience. They may have a will derived from nature and augmented by training, but such a power of mind is not a spiritual force, neither is it comparable to human will, inasmuch as it is not reflective— it is not the result of discriminating higher and moral meaning or choosing spiritual and eternal values. It is the possession of such power of spiritual discrimination and truth choosing that makes mortal man a moral being, a creature endowed with the attributes of spiritual responsibilities and the potential of survival."[5]* In other words it is the absence of mental powers in the animal which make it forever impossible for it to develop language or to experience anything that would equal personality survival in eternity. After this information, Ganid never again believed in the transmigration of the soul of man into the body of animals.

While Jesus was in Rome he gave many lecture and counsel many truth seeker. One evening while Jesus and his young student Ganid were leisurely strolling about Corinth near where the wall of the citadel ran down to the sea, they were approached by two public women. Ganid was of high standards; he detested everything that was unclean or evil; Ganid spoke to these women with great disrespect, and rudely motioned them away. Jesus, seeing this, said to Ganid: "You mean well, but you shouldn't speak to the children of God in such manner even though they may be erring children. Who are we to sit in judgment of these women? Do we understand the circumstances that led them to depend on such methods for their livelihood? Jesus said to his young friend, "Stop here that we may talk about these things." The crowd that was gathering around was more astonished than was Ganid. As they stood under the blanket of the moon, Jesus went on to say that there lives within every human a divine spirit, a gift of the Father in heaven. This good spirit ever strives to lead us to good.

Gonod and his son Ganid brought so many things in Alexandria and Rome that they sent all of their purchase ahead by pack train to Tarentum, while the three travelers walked leisurely across Italy over the great Apian way. While on this journey, they met all sorts of human beings. They encountered noble Roman citizens and Greek colonists that lived along this road and the progeny of a great number of less fortunate slaves were beginning to make their appearance.

One day while resting for lunch, they were about half way to Tarentum; Ganid asked Jesus about his thoughts on the caste system in India. Jesus said: "Though humans differ in many ways, the one from another, before God and in the spiritual world all mortal stands on an equal footing. There are only two groups of mortals in the eyes of God: Those who desire to do his will and those that do not."

When Jesus left Rome, he said nothing to any of his friends. The scribe of Damascus appeared in Rome without being announced and disappeared in the same way. It was a full year before they gave up hope of seeing him again. But by the end of the second year, those that knew him found themselves drawn together by their common interest in his teachings. They started to form small groups and continue to hold irregular and informal meetings right up to the time of the appearance of a preacher of the Christian religion in Rome.

After the trip to the Mediterranean, Jesus returned by way of Ur to Babylon were he joined a great caravan on its way to Damascus and from there, to Nazareth he stopped a few hours at Capernaum where he visited the Zebedee family. His brother James was there, who had sometime before took Jesus' place working at Zebedee's boat-shop. John Zebedee managed to buy a small house for Jesus with the funds Jesus had accumulated; Jesus turned the house over to James. Jesus stayed a few weeks in Nazareth and visited with family and friends. He spent some time at the repair shop with his brother Joseph, but he devoted most of his attention to his sister Mary and Ruth. Ruth, the youngest, was nearly fifteen years old and this was Jesus' chance to have a long talk with her since she had become a young lady. Both Jesus' Brothers Simon and Jude wanted to get married for sometimes now. But they didn't want to do this without Jesus' consent. So, they postpone getting married, hoping their oldest brother would return. Soon afterward, they had a double wedding.

Jesus visited with each individual member of his family and had a normal relationship, but when they were all together, he didn't have much to say. They talked about this among themselves; Mary was frustrated by this peculiar behavior of her first-born son.

Just about the time Jesus was considering leaving Nazareth, the leader of a very large caravan that was passing through the city became very sick. Jesus, being a linguist, volunteered to take his place. This trip would take him about a year and being that all of his brothers were married and his mother was living at home with Ruth, Jesus called a family conference and suggested that his mother and his youngest sister Ruth go to Capernaum to live in the house with James. It was agreed, and Joseph and his family moved into the Nazareth home.

The Caravan Trip to the Caspian Sea

Jesus started this caravan trip to Caspian Sea on the first of April A.D. 24. The caravan that Jesus joined as its conductor was going from Jerusalem to Damascus and then to Lake Urmia to Assyria, Media and Parthia to the southeastern Caspian Sea region. It would be a year before Jesus would return from this journey.

For Jesus, this trip was another one of exploration and personal ministry. He had an interesting experience with the entire caravan group. The many men, women and children who were in the caravan, lived better lives after this experience.

This was a very interesting episode in Jesus' life. He functioned during this year in an executive capacity, being responsible for material in his care and for the safe conduct of those travelers making up the caravan group; and he faithfully administered his duties.

When Jesus returned home from his trip to the Caspian Sea, he knew that his world travels was just about over; so he made one more trip to Syria. Jesus was thirty-one years old. After spending some time in the area of Caesarea, Philippi, he gather supplies, buying a mule and hiring a lad named Tiglath, and went by way of the Damascus road to a village some called Beit Jenn, in the foothills of Mount Hermon. Here near the middle of August A.D. 25, Jesus established his headquarters.

Tiglath went with Jesus the first day he ascended the slopes of the mountain to a designated point about 6,000 feet above sea level; there, he and Tiglath built a stone container; this is where Tiglath was to place Jesus' food twice a week.

The first day after he had left Tiglath, Jesus had ascended the mountain just a short distance when he paused to pray. Among other things, he asked the Father to send back the guardian seraphim to "be with Tiglath." He asked if he could be allowed to face up to his last struggles with the realities of mortal existence alone. The Father granted his request. He went into this great test with only his indwelling Adjuster (the God within) to guide and sustained him.

Jesus ate sparingly while on the mountain; he abstained from all food only a day or two at a time. This was where Jesus struggle with the superhuman beings that were his archenemies; these were beings that led the rebellion in the heaven worlds: Lucifer, Satan, and the prince of this world that is called Caligastia in the higher worlds. We, in the Christian world, call Lucifer Satan, but they are two different beings: Satan was Lucifer's second in command before the rebellion when Lucifer was in charge of 1,000 planets. (This information I gleaned from *The Urantia Book*. There are many things far beyond our understanding at this stage of our development, but these things can be learned.) Through the years somehow, Lucifer and Satan got mixed up as many things became distorted.

This is the time Jesus wrestled in spirit and defeated those archenemies. This struggle is recorded in the *Bible* as the last temptation Matthew 4:3-11. Jesus spent the last three weeks in August and the first three weeks in September on Mount Hermon. During these weeks, he finished the mortal task of achieving the circles of mind-understanding and personality control. During the last week of this period is also when Jesus faced his tempters and the *Bible* says defeated them. In short it was during this time Jesus came to the realization of who he really was. This temptation wasn't about food, temple pinnacles or kingdoms of this world, but the sovereignty of a mighty and glorious universe.

This section I will quote for the benefit of the reader: *"On an afternoon in late summer, amid the trees and in the silence of nature, Michael of Nebadon (Jesus Christ) won the unquestioned sovereignty of his universe. On that day he completed the task set for Creator Sons to live to the full the incarnated life in the likeness of mortal flesh on the evolutionary worlds of time and space. The universe announcement of this momentous achievement was not made until the day of his baptism, months afterward, but it all really took place that day on the mountain. And when Jesus came down from his sojourn on Mount Hermon, the Lucifer rebellion in Satania and the Caligastia secession on Urantia were virtually settled. Jesus had paid the last price required of him to attain the sovereignty of his universe, which in itself regulates the status of all rebels and determines that all such future upheavals (if they ever occur) may be dealt with summarily and effectively. Accordingly, it may be seen that the so-called "great temptation" of Jesus took place sometime before his baptism and not just after that event.*

At the end of this sojourn on the mountain, as Jesus was making his descent, he met Tiglath coming up to the rendezvous with food. Turning him back, he said only: "The period of rest is over; I must return to my Father's business." He was a silent and much changed man as they journeyed back to Dan, where he took leave of the lad, giving him the donkey. He then proceeded south by the same way he had come, to Capernaum.[6]

Jesus achieved the goal of his incarnation and became sovereign of Nebadon (our local universe). I know all of this seems strange, but this information was given to mankind several times throughout history; you can find vestiges of this information in the Hindu philosophy, one of the oldest religions in the world. I am sure we could have found information of this nature in the Alexandrian Library before its destruction. This kind of information was left behind by Adam, Eve and the Melchizidek. There is practically no information about the heaven worlds in Western Civilization. On the Sumerians cuneiform, you can also find traces about the heaven worlds.

I believe this information is given to us again through *The Urantia Book.* Are we going to ignore it until it's so badly distorted we won't be able to understand it? *The Urantia Book* is a difficult book to understand, even for people of today. Our ancient ancestors could not understand that information, but the Higher Beings continue to try. That's how much they love us.

At this point, I believe I have given enough information to show that Jesus had lived a life like most of us have a life of trials and tribulations. Now, I think I'll fast forward the scenery in my mind's eye to the time that Jesus began his ministry. There is a lot more to this story as I mentioned before. There are about seven hundred pages in the section on Jesus in *The Urantia Book.* In fact again space will not allow me to continue to give almost every detail.

CHAPTER 4

John the Baptist

According to *The Urantia Book*, John the Baptist was born March 25, B.C. 7, just as Gabriel had promised Elizabeth in June of the year before. For five months, Elizabeth kept Gabriel's visit a secret. Zacharias was leery of the story when Elizabeth told him about it, and didn't fully believe it until after he had a strange dream, just as Jesus' father had. Except for the visit of Gabriel, there was nothing unreal or supernatural connected to the birth of John the Baptist. Both John and Jesus had human fathers. I suppose if Elizabeth and Zacharias had not been married for such a long time, the Roman Catholic Church would have said that John was born of a virgin, that his birth was supernatural. When Gabriel announced the birth, he didn't say anything about one being born differently than the other. So where did the Romans get their fantastic story from. If the story was from the Old Testament, why didn't Gabriel announce that? It would have been extremely important if it was true, but he just said two sons would be born.

The most eventful thing that happened in John's early life was when his parents took him to see Jesus and his family. This visit took place in the month of June B.C. 1, John was a little over six years old. When he returned home his parents began to educate him; there was no synagogue school in this little village. Zacharias, being a priest, was fairly educated and Elizabeth was better educated than the average Judean women; since John was the only child, they spent a great amount of time on his spiritual and mental training. (Otherwise, he grew up as an ordinary child in a small city known in those days as the city of Judah about four miles from Jerusalem.)

John Becomes a Nazarite

John had no school from which to graduate at age fourteen; his parents decided that this was the appropriate time for him to take the formal Nazarite vow. So, Zacharias and Elizabeth took their son to Engedi down by the Dead Sea. Here, was the southern headquarters of the Nazarite Brotherhood, and here, John was inducted into this order for life. In this order, one had to abstain from all intoxicating drinks, let their hair grow long, and refrain from touching the dead. After John made his vow, the family went to Jerusalem, where before the temple, John had to finalize the making of the offering which was required of those taking the Nazarite vow.

The vow John took was the same vow that his famous predecessors, Samson and the prophet Samuel, took. A Nazarite was considered a sanctified and holy person. The Jews looked upon the Nazarite with almost the same respect and honor that is given to a high priest; for them, it was not strange for the Nazarites of lifelong consecration to be the only persons except the high priests that was permitted to enter the holy of holies in the temples.

When John was sixteen years old, as a result of reading about Elijah, he became very impressed with the prophet of Mount Camel and decided to adopt his style of dress. From that day on, John always wore a hairy garment with a leather girdle. At sixteen, John was more than six feet tall and almost full grown. With his flowing hair and strange mode of dress, he was certainly an odd looking youth. His parents expected great things of their only son, a child of promise and a Nazarite for life.

In the beginning of the month of March, A.D. 25, John traveled around the western coast of the Dead Sea and up the river Jordan opposite of Jericho, the ancient ford over which Joshua and the children of Israel had passed when they first entered the Promised Land. He crossed over to the other side of the river; he prepared himself near the entrance of the ford and began to preach to the people on their way to and fro across the river. As this is where most people crossed.

It was recognized by all who heard John that he was more than just a preacher. Most people who listened to this weird man, who came up from the Judean wilderness, went away believing they had heard the voice of a prophet. Tens of thousands of listeners came to hear him, some curious, but many in earnest and serious as they came from all parts of Judea, Perea and Samaria. The souls of these weary and expectant Jews were greatly stirred by this phenomenon. Not in all of their history had the devout children of Abraham longed for *"Consolation of Israel"* or more faintly looked for *"the restoration of the kingdom."* Not in all Jewish history could John's message, *"The kingdom of heaven is at hand,"* have more of a universal appeal as the very time he mysteriously appeared at the bank of the crossing of the Jordan. *"He was dressed like Elijah of old, and he thundered his admonition and poured forth his warning in the spirit and power of Elijah," The Urantia Book.*

By December of A.D. 25, John's fame extended throughout all of Palestine; his work was the conversation of the entire town about the lake of Galilee. Jesus, speaking favorably of John's message, caused many from Capernaum to join John's cult of repentance and baptism. James and John, the sons of Zebedee, had gone in December to see John. After that, they went down once a week and brought back first hand reports of the evangelist's work to Jesus.

Two of Jesus' brothers, James and Jude, had talked about going down to John to be baptized. Jude had come over to Capernaum for the Sabbath service; he and James, after listening to Jesus' discourse in the synagogue, decided to talk to Jesus about their plans for baptism by John. This was on a Saturday, January 12, A.D. 26. Jesus asked them if they would postpone the discussion until the following day and he would give them his answer.

Jesus slept very little that night; he was in close intercourse with the Father in heaven. He arranged to have lunch with his brothers at noon that next day, and then he would advise them concerning their desire to be baptized by John. That Sunday, Jesus was working as usual in the boat-shop. James and Jude had arrived with his lunch and were waiting in the lumber room for him. It was not yet time for the midday break, and they knew that their brother Jesus was very prompt about such matters.

A little before noon rest, Jesus laid down his tools, removed his work apron, and said to the three workmen that were in the room with him," My hour has come." He went out to the lumber room where his brothers were waiting, repeating, "My hour has come let us go to John" *The Urantia Book*. And they started right away to Pella where John was preaching and baptizing, eating their lunch on the way. This was Sunday, January 13. They stayed for the night in the Jordan Valley and arrived where John was baptizing around noon of the next day.

The Baptism of Jesus

John had just started baptizing the aspirants for the day. Many repentant were standing in line waiting their turn to be baptized when Jesus and his brothers got in line with these earnest men and women who had become believes in John's teachings concerning the coming kingdom.

John had asked about Jesus' several times when he talked to Zebedee's sons. He heard of Jesus remarks about his preaching and day by day, he was hoping to see him arrive on the scene, but he did not expect to greet him in line with the baptism candidates. In fact, John was engrossed with the details of baptizing a large number of converts that he didn't see Jesus, the "Son of Man," until he was in his immediate presence. After recognizing Jesus, the ceremony was halted for a moment as John greeted his cousin, and asked, *"But why did you come down into the water to greet me?"*

And Jesus answered, *"To be subject to your baptism."*

John answered: *"But I have need to be baptized by you. Why do you come to me?"*

And Jesus whispered to John: "Bear with me now, for it becomes us to set example for my brothers standing here with me and that the people would know that my hour has come." [1]

Jesus spoke to John with a voice of authority. John was trembling with emotion as he prepared Jesus of Nazareth in the Jordan River at noon on Monday, January 14, A.D. 26. And so John baptized Jesus and his two brothers, James and Jude. And when John baptized these three, he dismissed the crowd for the day, telling them he would resume baptism the next day at noon. As the people went on their way, the four men still standing in the water, heard a strange sound and their appeared for a moment an apparition over the head of Jesus and they heard a voice saying, "This is my beloved Son in whom I am well pleased." A tremendous change came over the face of Jesus; he got out of the water in silence and took his leave of them, going toward the hills to the east. And no man saw Jesus again for forty days.

When Jesus walked away, John followed him for a distance to tell him of the story of Gabriel's visit to his mother before either of them was born. John said he had heard the story so many times from his mother's lips. He let Jesus continue on his way after he said; "Now I know of a certainty that you are the Deliverer." But Jesus said nothing.

During the time of those forty days of waiting, many rumors spread throughout the countryside all the way to Tiberias and Jerusalem. Thousands went over to see the new attraction in John's camp. They talked about the Messiah, but Jesus was nowhere to be seen. When the disciples of John claim that the strange man of God took to the hills, many doubted the whole story.

Around three weeks after Jesus went to the hills, there appeared on the scene at Pella deputies from the priests and Pharisees at Jerusalem. They asked John on the spot if he was Elijah or the prophet that Moses had promised, and John said,

"I am not." Then they ask, *"Are you the Messiah?"*

John answered, *"I am not."* Then asked them from Jerusalem "If you are not the prophet, nor the Messiah, then who gave you the right to baptize people and create such a stir?"

John said, *"It is up to those people that have heard me and received my baptism to announce who I am."* Then he said, *"Although I baptize with water, there has been among us one who will return and baptize you with the Holy Spirit."[2]*

These were arduous days in John's experience; he had prayed for Jesus return. Some of John's disciples organized groups to go in search of Jesus, but John forbade them, saying: *"Our times are in the hands of the God of heaven; he will direct his chosen Son,"* The Urantia Book.

The Forty Days

Jesus had overcome the Great Temptation of his mortal initiation before his baptism when he was on Mount Hermon for six weeks. He had gone into forty days of rest to formulate the plans for proclaiming the new Kingdom of God in the hearts of man. Jesus did not go into the hills for the purpose of fasting and the affliction of his soul. He was not an ascetic, and he came to eradicate all such belief, regarding the search for God.

Jesus was then fully self-conscious concerning his relation to the universe of his making and his many helpers;

he was also aware of the universe of universes controlled by God the Father in heaven. He now recalls the instruction give to him by his older brother Immanuel before he entered upon his earth incarnation. He clearly understood all relationships and he wanted to be away for awhile and meditate, to think out his plans for public service.

While Jesus was wandering about the hills looking for suitable shelter, he encountered his universe chief of staff, Gabriel, the Bright and Morning Star of Nebadon, (our local universe). Gabriel re-established personal communication with the Creator Son of our universe now Jesus of Nazareth; they met directly for the first time since Michael (Jesus) left Gabriel in the higher worlds in preparation for his final initiation on earth. Gabriel informed Jesus that his experience on earth was practically over, as far as concerned, his earning the title of sovereignty ruler of our universe and the termination of Lucifer rebellion. *"And Jesus came and spoke unto them saying All power is given unto me in heaven and in earth" Matthew 28:18.*

Another Higher Being joined Jesus and Gabriel in their conference; he told Jesus he was now at liberty to terminate his incarnation, to ascend to the right hand of the Father to receive sovereignty rights and take over his well earned unconditional ruler-ship of all Nebadon. Meanwhile through all of the forty days Jesus was away, James and John Zebedee were searching for him. Several times they were not far from the place he had chosen as his shelter, but they never found him.

Jesus wasn't ready to return to the higher worlds, even though he was granted permission to do so. He couldn't leave his sons and daughters on earth without demonstrating to them the reason for being. He came that we may live life more fully. Part of his demonstration was to die and in three days, rise again. How often did he tell the Pharisees, if you destroy this temple (his body) in three, I'll raise it up again John 2:19. By dying and raising his body in three days, he was demonstrating to us that life is a continuum. After our transition, we will continue to evolve.

Jesus also said in my Father's house are many mansions, and I go to prepare a place for you John 14:2. He said his kingdom is not of this world John 18:36. Wasn't he telling us there are other worlds? Jesus was free to return to the worlds from whence he came and have complete dominion over his universe. But he loved mankind so much he was willing to die to show us that life is a continuum; he was willing to go through all the suffering to prove it to us. Today in physics the physicists are on the verge of proving there are other dimensions that are teeming with life.

On the Sabbath February 23, A.D. 26, at morning breakfast, the group that was with John looked up toward the north and saw Jesus coming towards them. As he approached, John stood upon a large rock and lifting his voice, said: "Behold the Son of God, the deliverer of the world; this is the one of whom I spoke of; after me, there will come one who is preferred because he was before me; for this reason I came out of the wilderness to preach repentance and to be baptized with water announcing the kingdom of heaven is at hand. Now the one is here who will baptize you with the Holy Spirit. And I saw the Divine Spirit descending upon this man, and I heard the voice of God declare, *"This is my beloved Son in whom I am well pleased."*

Jesus asked them to return to their meal, while he sat down to eat with John for his brothers had returned to Capernaum.

All that Sabbath day, February 23, Jesus mingled with the people that surrounded John's camp. He ministered to a small boy who injured himself in a fall, and he took the child home to a nearby village in Pella to make sure the boy got safely home to his parents. During that Sabbath, two of John's most important disciples spent a lot of time with Jesus; they were Andrew and his brother Simon; Andrew went with Jesus to make sure the boy got home safe as well.

The Real Jesus

Andrew was profoundly impressed with Jesus' teachings; on the way back to John's camp he asked Jesus many questions. Andrew said to Jesus, *"I have watched you every since you came to Capernaum and I believe you are the new teacher; although I do not understand all your teachings, I have made up my mind to follow you. I will sit at your feet and learn the whole truth about your new kingdom of God"* *The Urantia Book.* Andrew was the first of Jesus' twelve apostles who was to work with Jesus in the establishment of the new Kingdom of God in the hearts of men.

Jesus had returned to Pella for the night; Andrew and Simon were discussing the nature of their involvement in the establishment of the coming kingdom when James and John the sons of Zebedee arrived; they were just returning from the hills in search of Jesus; when they approached John the Baptist's camp, they overheard Simon Peter and his brother Andrew talking about their acceptance as Jesus' apostles and that they were leaving for Galilee the next morning. James and John were sad; they had known Jesus for some time and had lived with him. They searched for him in the hills many days, only to return to learn others had been selected before them as his apostles. They asked where was Jesus and they made haste to find him.

Jesus was asleep when they located him; they awakened him asking, "How is it that we who have so long lived with you and while we search the hills for you, you choose Andrew and Simon before us as your apostles in the new kingdom? "Jesus told them to be calm" and ask yourself. Who asked you to search for me while I was about my Father business?" Jesus told them they should search for the secret of the kingdom in their hearts and not in the hills. John was bold enough to ask, "Master, will James and I be associates of yours in the new kingdom as Andrew and Simon?" Jesus' answer was so touching, I will quote it:

And Jesus, laying a hand on the shoulder of each of them, said:*" My brethren, you were already with me in the spirit of the kingdom, even before these others made request to be received. You, my brethren, have no need to make request for entrance into the kingdom; you have been with me in the kingdom from the beginning. Before men, others may take precedence over you, but in my heart, did I also number you in the councils of the kingdom, even before you thought to make this request of me. And even so might you have been first before men had you not been absent engaged in a well-intentioned, but self-appointed task of seeking for one who was not lost. In the coming kingdom, be not mindful of those things which foster your anxiety, but rather at all times concern yourselves only with doing the will of the Father who is in heaven."* [3]

Early that next morning, Jesus left John and his disciples going back to Galilee; he never said when he would see them again. John asked about his own preaching and mission. Jesus only said, *"My Father will guide you now and in the future as he has in the past."* And these great men separated that morning, on the banks of the Jordan River, never to see each other again in the flesh.

After Jesus left John's camp on his way to Galilee, he asked the four that he had already chosen as apostles to help select the other eight and they did until there were twelve of them. Not long after that, John the Baptist was imprisoned and was killed by Herod Antipas.

CHAPTER 5

The Wedding at Cana

Now we will fast forward to a wedding Jesus was invited to and the so called miracle of the wine. This period of history in the Middle East, especially among the Jews, people always expected prophets or messiahs to perform great wonders to prove that they are of God. But Jesus didn't believe this proved anything; he didn't like to disrupt the laws of nature. He did wonderful things, but usually they were within the laws of nature in some way we don't understand. Jesus' mother and family always expected him to perform some kind of miracle, but he had always refused.

This was an important wedding Jesus was invited too; his mother and most of his brothers and sisters were there. A great multitude of people were there as well, many of whom were not invited, and they soon ran out of wine. Those people that were not invited were there because Jesus led the wedding procession and he was becoming very well known in that area; he had performed quite a few healings.

Jesus was by, this time, completely aware regarding his human existence, his divine per-existence and the state of his combined, human or fused, human and divine natures.

As the wedding day progressed, Jesus became more conscious that the people expected him to perform some kind of miracle, especially his family who were looking for him to announce his coming kingdom by some startling and super-natural manifestation. Jesus' family and the apostles expected Jesus to sit on the throne of David, gather an army and crush their Roman oppressors. But Jesus came to earth (the higher ones call Urantia) as the prince of peace.

Early in the afternoon at the wedding Mary Jesus' mother went and found her son James; together, they went and approached Jesus to ask him at what hour he had planned to make himself known as the "Supernatural One." Jesus said, "If you love me, then be willing to wait, while I wait upon the will of my Father in heaven." This act of his mother was a disappointment to the human Jesus. When Jesus was in the hills deciding how he would go about presenting God's kingdom to humanity, he decided against outward demonstration of his divinity. For several hours, Mary was depressed. She said to James, "I don't understand him. Is there no end to his strange ways?"

The wedding proceeded with a silence of expectation. Then, the word went around that the carpenter and boat builder, announced by John the Baptist as "The Deliverer," will show his hand during the evening festivities, perhaps at the wedding supper. But all expectance of supernatural demonstration was removed from the apostles when Jesus called them together. He said to them, *"Think not that I have come to this place to work some wonder for the gratification of the curious or for the conviction of those who doubt. Rather are we here to wait upon the will of our Father who art in heaven."* When Mary and other, saw him gathering with his apostles, they reached the conclusion something awesome was about to happen. They all sat down to enjoy the wedding supper and evening festivities in great expectation.

The father of the bridegroom purchased enough wine for all that was invited to the wedding; how was he to know that the marriage of his son would be an event so closely related to the expected announcement of Jesus as the "Messianic Deliverer," and people would invite themselves. He was delighted to have Jesus as his honored guest. But little before the wedding supper was over; one of the servants brought him the bad news that the wine was running low.

The Real Jesus

When supper ended the guests were strolling about the garden; the mother of the bridegroom informed Mary, Jesus' mother that the supply of wine had run out. Mary told her not to worry that she will speak to her son, and she said, *"He will help us."* This section is so touching; I felt I would be justified in quoting it:

"Throughout a period of many years, Mary had always turned to Jesus for help in every crisis of their home life at Nazareth, so that it was only natural for her to think of him at this time. But this ambitious mother had still other motives for appealing to her eldest son on this occasion. As Jesus was standing alone in a corner of the garden, his mother approached him, saying, "My son, they have no wine." And Jesus answered, "My good woman, what have I to do with that?" Said Mary, "But I believe your hour has come; cannot you help us?" Jesus replied: "Again I declare that I have not come to do things in this wise. Why do you trouble me again with these matters?" And then, breaking down in tears, Mary entreated him, "But, my son, I promised them that you would help us; won't you please do something for me?" And then spoke Jesus: "Woman, what have you to do with making such promises? See that you do it not again. We must in all things wait upon the will of the Father in heaven."

Mary, the mother of Jesus, was crushed; she was stunned! As she stood there before him motionless, with the tears streaming down her face, the human heart of Jesus was overcome with compassion for the woman who had borne him in the flesh; and bending forward, he laid his hand tenderly upon her head, saying: "Now, now, Mother Mary, grieve not over my apparently hard sayings, for have I not many times told you that I have come only to do the will of my heavenly Father? Most gladly would I do what you ask of me if it were a part of the Father's will —"and Jesus stopped short, he hesitated. Mary seemed to sense that something was happening. Leaping up, she threw her arms around

Jesus' neck, kissed him, and rushed off to the servants' quarters, saying, "Whatever my son says, that do." But Jesus said nothing. He now realized that he had already said — or rather desirefully thought — too much.

Mary was dancing with glee. She did not know how the wine would be produced, but she confidently believed that she had finally persuaded her first-born son to assert his authority, to dare to step forth and claim his position and exhibit his Messianic power. And, because of the presence and association of certain universe powers and personalities, of which all those present were wholly ignorant, she was not to be disappointed. The wine Mary desired and which Jesus, the God-man, humanly and sympathetically wished for, was forthcoming.

Near at hand stood six waterpots of stone, filled with water, holding about twenty gallons apiece. This water was intended for subsequent use in the final purification ceremonies of the wedding celebration. The commotion of the servants about these huge stone vessels, under the busy direction of his mother, attracted Jesus' attention, and going over, he observed that they were drawing wine out of them by the pitcherful.

It was gradually dawning upon Jesus what had happened. Of all persons present at the marriage feast of Cana, Jesus was the most surprised. Others had expected him to work a wonder, but that was just what he had purposed not to do. And then the Son of Man recalled the admonition of his Personalized Thought Adjuster in the hills. He recounted how the Adjuster had warned him about the inability of any power or personality to deprive him of the creator prerogative of independence of time. On this occasion power transformers, midwayers, and all other required personalities were assembled near the water and other necessary elements, and in the face of the expressed wish of the Universe Creator Sovereign, there was no escaping the instantaneous appearance of wine. And this occurrence was made doubly certain since the Personalized Adjuster had signified that the execution of the Son's desire was in no way a contravention of the Father's will."[1]

There was no hocus-pocus preformed here. Because of the compassion Jesus felt for his mother and his desire to help her, he activated what the scientists today are calling the zero-point-energy-field. His desire to help her was enough for those powerful beings in higher dimension to bring his desire into manifestation almost instantaneously. Usually, when we wish something into manifestation, it takes time and we have to be persistent. Jesus being a Creator Son, the Higher Beings, through the zero-point-energy-field, brought Jesus' desire into manifestation right away.

The zero-point-energy-field was discovered in the last century in the year 1913 by Albert Einstein and Otto Stern in Germany. This field is the lowest point of any energy system, such as an atom or electron. Scientists of today believe this energy can think in some ways, they are not able to understand yet. They believe this energy field is what fuels our DNA and our very being. I would imagine a spiritual person would call this field on our plane of being, "The mind of God."

In today's society, all over the world, new concepts on thoughts are springing-up; many books are being written about the power of thoughts. People are beginning to realize thoughts are energy, and this energy can create after its kind, good or bad. In other words, when we think, if there is enough energy behind it, it will manifest into the physical world. I wrote in depth about the zero-point-energy-field in my previous book, *Journey to Life*. Jesus' desire to help his mother, even though it was not his intention, activated the zero-point-energy-field and those Higher Beings made it happen instantaneously.

In the *Bible,* there is another place that Jesus mentions the zero-point-energy-field, although he didn't call it that. Mark: 22-24 states: *"And Jesus answering saith unto them,*

"Have faith in God. For verily I say unto you, that whosoever shall say unto this mountain, be thou removed, and 'be thou cast into the sea;' and shall not doubt in his heart, but shall believe that those things which he saith shall come to pass; he shall have whatsoever he saith. Therefore I say unto you, what things soever ye desire, when ye pray believe that ye receive them, and ye shall have them."

Two thousand years ago Jesus was using this energy field and we are just beginning to understand it. Some people say Jesus was just another man, but I don't think so. He is a higher Son of God who incarnated into a human embryo just as our essence has done for thousands of years.

People in the past always say that religion and science don't go together. When will they learn that God and the Higher Beings are the ultimate scientists? There are no greater scientists.

God's Wrath

During the month of April A.D. 26 Jesus and the Apostles worked in Jerusalem ministering to the people; this was the month of the Passover Festivities. There was a man attending the Passover Festivities by the name of Jacob he was a wealthy Jewish trader from Crete, and he came to Andrew one of Jesus' apostles, requesting to see Jesus privately. Andrew arranged this meeting with Jesus at the home of one called Flavius' the evening of the next day. This man could not understand Jesus' teaching and desired to understand it better; he wanted to know more about the kingdom of God.

The next day at Flavius' home, Jacob said to Jesus: *"But Rabbi Moses and the olden prophets tells us that Yahweh is a jealous God, a God of great wrath and fierce anger. The prophets said he hates evildoers and takes vengeance on those that obey not his law. You and your disciples tells us that God is a kind and compassionate*

Father who loves all men that he would welcome into his new kingdom of heaven which you proclaim is so near at hand.

When Jacob finished speaking, Jesus said: *"Jacob, you well stated the teaching of the olden prophets who taught the children of their generation in accordance with the light of their day. Our Father in Paradise is changeless. But the concept of his nature has enlarged and grown from the days of Moses down through the days of Amos and even to the generation of the prophet Isaiah. And now have I come in the flesh to reveal the Father in the new glory, and to show forth his love and mercy to all men on all worlds. As the gospel of this kingdom shall spread over the world with its message of good cheer and good will to all men, there will grow up improved and better relations among families of all nations. As time passes, father and children will love each other more, and thus will be brought about a better understanding of the love of the Father in heaven for his children on earth. Remember Jacob that a good and true father not only loves his family as a whole—as a family—butt he also truly loves and affectionately cares for each individual member."*

After talking for a while about the Father's character, Jesus paused and said to Jacob, *"You being the father of many knows what I am saying are true."* Jacob said to Jesus, *"But who told you that I am the father of six children? How did you know this about me?"* And Jesus said, *"Suffice it to say that the Father and the Son knows all things, for indeed they see all. Loving your children as a father on earth, you must now accept as a reality the love of the heavenly Father for you—not just all the children of Abraham, but for you, your individual soul.*

Then Jesus went on to say: *"When your children are very young and immature, and you must chastise them, they may reflect that their father is angry and filled with resentful wrath. Their immaturity cannot penetrate beyond the punishment to discern the father's farseeing and corrective affection. But when these same children become grown-up-men and women, would it not be folly for them to cling to these earlier and misconceived notions regarding their father? As men and women, they should now discern their father's love in all these disciplines. And should not mankind, as the centuries pass, come the better to understand the true nature and loving character of the Father in heaven. What profit have you from successive generations of spiritual illumination if you persist in viewing God as Moses and the prophets saw him? I say to you, Jacob, under the bright light of this hour you should see the Father as none of those who have gone before ever beheld him. And thus seeing him, you should rejoice to enter the kingdom wherein such a merciful Father rules, and you should seek to have his will of love dominate your life henceforth."*

And Jacob answered: *"Rabbi I believe, I desire that you lead me into the Father Kingdom."²*

The Purpose of Affliction

One of the private interviews Jesus held in Zebedee's garden was with Nathaniel, one of his twelve apostles. At another of these private interviews in the garden, Nathaniel asked Jesus: "Master, though I am beginning to understand why you refuse to practice healing indiscriminately, I am still at a loss to understand why the loving Father in heaven permits so many of his children on earth to suffer so many afflictions." The Master answered Nathaniel, saying:

"Nathaniel, you and many others are thus perplexed because you do not comprehend how the natural order of this world has been so many times upset by the sinful adventures of certain rebellious traitors to the Father's will. And I have come to make a beginning of setting these things in order. But many ages will be required to restore this part of the universe to former paths and thus release the children

The Real Jesus

of men from the extra burdens of sin and rebellion. The presence of evil alone is sufficient test for the ascension of man — sin is not essential to survival.

But, my son, you should know that the Father does not purposely afflict his children. Man brings down upon himself unnecessary affliction as a result of his persistent refusal to walk in the better ways of the divine will. Affliction is potential in evil, but much of it has been produced by sin and iniquity. Many unusual events have transpired on this world, and it is not strange that all thinking men should be perplexed by the scenes of suffering and affliction which they witness. But of one thing you may be sure: The Father does not send affliction as an arbitrary punishment for wrongdoing. The imperfections and handicaps of evil are inherent; the penalties of sin are inevitable; the destroying consequences of iniquity are inexorable. Man should not blame God for those afflictions which are the natural result of the life which he chooses to live; neither should man complain of those experiences which are a part of life as it is lived on this world. It is the Father's will that mortal man should work persistently and consistently toward the betterment of his estate on earth. Intelligent application would enable man to overcome much of his earthly misery.

"Nathaniel, it is our mission to help men solve their spiritual problems and in this way to quicken their minds so that they may be the better prepared and inspired to go about solving their manifold material problems. I know of your confusion as you have read the Scriptures. All too often there has prevailed a tendency to ascribe to God the responsibility for everything which ignorant man fails to understand. The Father is not personally responsible for all you may fail to comprehend. Do not doubt the love of the Father just because some just and wise law of his ordaining chances to afflict you because you have innocently or deliberately transgressed such a divine ordinance."[3]

I mentioned before that the rebellion of the prince of this world and Lucifer, which Jesus spoke of also the default of Adam and Eve, caused great suffering on our planet. Jesus mentions in this quote that the imperfection and handicaps of evil are inherent, but it is now known that we can change our disposition; I quote from my previous book, *Journey to Life*. "And recently scientists have discovered that we can alter our DNA in a much shorter period than previously believed; the workings of the genes are not carved in stone. A well known doctor named Bruce Lipton in his book, *The Biology of Life*, shows that our beliefs, true or false, positive or negative, affect genetic activity and actually alters our genetic code. And all this coincides with God's plan of free will. We can no longer blame our genes for what happened to us. We can blame ourselves."[4]

Jesus also states that it is the Father's will that mortal man should work persistently and consistently toward the betterment of his estate on earth. He says that intelligent application would enable man to overcome much of his misery. We can, if we are persistent, overcome. Many people do overcome; you can read my autobiography, *Hard Times Don't Last Always,* and learn what I had to overcome as an abused child.

The Discourse on True Religion

"The religion of the physical senses superstitious fear of natural man, the Master refused to belittle, though he deplored the fact that so much of this primitive form of worship should persist in the religious forms of the more intelligent races of mankind. Jesus made it clear that the great difference between the religion of the mind and the religion of the spirit is that, while the former is upheld by ecclesiastical authority, the latter is wholly based on human experience.

Until the race becomes highly intelligent and more fully civilized, there will persist many of those childlike and superstitious ceremonies which are so characteristics of evolutionary religious practice of primitive and backward people. Until the human race progresses to the level of a higher and more general recognition of the realities of spiritual experience, large numbers of men and women will continue to show a personal preference for those religion of authority which require only intellectual assent, in contrast to the religion of the spirit, which entails active participation of mind and soul in the faith adventure of grappling with the rigorous realities of progressive human experience.

The acceptance of the traditional religions of authority presents the easy way out for man's urge to seek satisfaction for the longings of his spiritual nature. The settled, crystallized, and established religion of authority afford a ready refuge to which the distracted and distraught of man may flee when harassed by fear and tormented by uncertainty. Such a religion requires of its devotees, as the price to be paid for its satisfaction and assurances, only a passive and purely intellectual assent.

And for a long time there will live on earth those timid, fearful, and hesitant individuals who will prefer thus to secure religious consolations, even though, in so casting their lot with the religion of authority, they compromise the sovereignty of personality, debase the dignity of self-respect, and utterly surrender the right to participate in the most thrilling and inspiring of all possible human experience: the personal quest for truth, the exhilaration of facing the perils of intellectual discovery, the determination to explore the realities of personal religious experience, the supreme satisfaction of experiencing the personal triumph of actual realization of victory of spiritual faith over intellectual doubt as it is honestly won in the supreme adventure of all human experience—man seeking God, for himself and as himself and finding him.

The religion of the spirit means effort, struggle, conflict, faith, determination, love, loyalty and progress. The religion of the mind—the theology and authority—requires little or none of these exertions from its formal believers. Tradition is a safe refuge and an easy path for those fearful and halfhearted souls who instinctively shun the spirit struggles and mental uncertainties associated with those faith voyages of daring adventure out upon the high sea of unexplored truth in search for the farther shores of spiritual realities as they may be discovered by the progressive human mind and experienced by the evolving soul. "[5]

Jesus is telling us, that we have to participate in developing our own spirituality; we need to saturate our souls with the spirit of God, and not to depend on the religion of authority. We need to find God, through our own efforts. There are many things Jesus said that are not in the *Bible*; and you know the Churches would not allow the statement from above to be placed in the *Bible*. *"And there are many other things Jesus did, that which, if they should be written every one, I suppose that even the world itself could not contain the books that should be written"* (John 21:25).

Resurrection of Lazarus

Very late Sunday night, February 26, A.D. 30, a runner from a small village called Bethany arrived at Philadelphia where Jesus and his apostles were ministering to the people with a message from Lazarus's sisters, Martha and Mary, saying:*" Lord, him whom you love is very sick."*

Jesus sent a message back saying: *"This sickness is not to the death. Doubt not that it may be used to glorify the Father and exalts the Son."* Jesus was very fond of Mary, Martha and their brother Lazarus. Jesus arrived in Bethany where Lazarus was four days after his death. Of all of Jesus' healing and restoring sight to the blind, his greatest work was the raising of Lazarus from the dead.

As I said before there was no hocus-pocus going on. When Jesus reached the place where Lazarus was buried, a small group of Lazarus's friends gathered around. The people present at the burial site didn't realize the presence of a vast array of celestial beings at hand, in another dimension being assembled under the leadership of Gabriel and just waiting to execute the biddings of their beloved sovereign, Jesus of Nazareth.

Jesus asked that the stone be moved from the entrance to the tomb where Lazarus laid. Martha didn't understand why Jesus wanted the stone moved; she thought perhaps Jesus wanted to see Lazarus one last time. They hesitated to roll away the stone. Jesus said, *"Did I not tell you this sickness is not to the death; if you just believe you would see the glory of God?"* When Jesus finished speaking his apostles, with the help of neighbors, moved the stone from the entrance to the tomb.

As a company of about 45 people stood at the tomb, they could barely see the form of Lazarus wrapped in linen bandages. While these earth people stood there in silence, a vest host of celestial beings had sprung into their place waiting to answer the signal to action given by Gabriel, their commander.

Jesus lifted up his eyes and said: *"Father I am thankful that you heard and answer my request. I know that you always hear me, but because of those that stand here with me, I thus speak with you, that they may believe that you have sent me into the world and that they may know that you are working with me in that which we are about to do."* And when he had prayed, he cried out with a loud voice, *"Lazarus come forth."*[6]

Although the humans didn't make a move, the vast celestial was all astir in unified action in obedience to the creators' word. In just twelve seconds (according to *"The Urantia Book)* of our time the before lifeless body of Lazarus began to move and sat up on the edge of the stone shelf where it had rested. His body was bonded with grave cloths and his face was covered with napkins. He stood up before them—alive Jesus said, *"Loose him and let him go; The Urantia Book."*

All but the apostles, Mary and Martha fled to the house. They were pale with fright and overcome with amazement. While some stayed, many hurried to their homes. Lazarus, standing there, greeted Jesus and the apostles and asked the meaning of the grave cloths, and why he had awakened in the garden. Jesus and the apostles moved to one side, while Martha told Lazarus of his death, burial and resurrection. She explained all that had happened to him.

Some may think this is a strange story, but if we were in existence for billions of years as some of those Higher Beings, what is there we wouldn't be able to do? Some of those beings that were present at the time of Lazarus' resurrection, no doubt helped to build the universe, that our scientists claims to be around 13.7 billion years old; someone had to create it. There was no hocus-pocus (smile).

"Then went Lazarus over to Jesus and, with his sisters, knelt at the Master's feet to give thanks and offer praise to God. Jesus, taking Lazarus by the hand, lifted him up, saying: "My son, what has happened to you will also be experienced by all who believe this gospel except that they shall be resurrected in a more glorious form. You shall be a living witness of the truth which I spoke — I am the resurrection and the life. But let us all now go into the house and partake of nourishment for these physical bodies."

As they walked toward the house, Gabriel dismissed the extra groups of the assembled heavenly host while he made record of the first instance on Urantia, and the last, where a mortal creature had been resurrected in the likeness of the physical body of death.

Lazarus could hardly comprehend what had occurred. He knew he had been very sick, but he could recall only that he had fallen asleep and been awakened. He was never able to tell anything about these four days in the tomb because he was wholly unconscious. Time is nonexistent to those who sleep the sleep of death.

Though many believed in Jesus as a result of this mighty work, others only hardened their hearts the more to reject him. By noon the next day this story had spread over all Jerusalem. Scores of men and women went to Bethany to look upon Lazarus and talk with him, and the alarmed and disconcerted Pharisees hastily called a meeting of the Sanhedrin that they might determine what should be done about these new developments.[7] "

When we make our transition, the same thing will happened to us that happen to Lazarus; he didn't realize he had died until his sister told him and he took up his life where he left off. The only difference is that we will be in another dimension with new bodies made of different material, we will continue our living.

CHAPTER 6

The Last Days of Jesus

When the work of teaching the people did not command their attention, the custom of Jesus and the apostles were to rest from all activities on Wednesdays. On this specific Wednesday, they ate breakfast later than usual and their camp was filled with an all consuming silence; little was said during the first half of breakfast. Jesus broke the silence by telling his apostles that he desired all of them to rest for the day, to take time to reflect on all that had happened since they had come to Jerusalem; also to think about what was just ahead.

After breakfast, the Master informed the apostle Andrew who was the administrator of their group that he planned to be absent for the day and suggested that the apostles be permitted to spend time according to their desires; but under no circumstance were they to go into Jerusalem.

When Jesus prepared to go into the hills alone, David Zebedee, one of Jesus' close friends, approached him; he told him that he well knew that the Pharisees and Rulers were out to destroy him, and *"you are preparing to go into the hills alone; I will send three men with you to make sure you are safe."* Jesus told David that he meant well, *"But you are wrong; you don't understand that no harm will come to me, until that hour when I am ready to lay down my life in conformity with my Father will; I need no one to go with me."*

There was a teenager named John Mark who hang around Jesus' camp; he always did errands for the group; he was around 16 years old. He walked up to Jesus with a basket of food and water, and suggested that if he planned on being away all day, he might become hungry. Jesus smiled at the lad and reached for the basket. John held onto the basket and saying, *"Master, you might stop to pray, forget and walk off and leave the basket; perhaps I can go along and hold the basket for you."* A group of people standing looked in astonishment as the young man held onto the basket; Jesus looked at the boy and said, *"Since with all your heart you crave to go with me, it shall not be denied you. We will go off by ourselves and have a good visit. You may ask me any question that arises in your heart, and we will comfort and console each other. You may start out carrying the lunch, and when you grow weary, I will help you. Follow on with me."*[1] Jesus was a kind and compassionate human beings. As they walked alone the path, Jesus mentioned to John that he would be a mighty messenger for the Kingdom of God.

Jesus did not return to the camp that day until after sunset. He spent this day of quiet on earth with this truth-seeking youth and talking with his Paradise Father. This event has became known in the higher worlds as the God of this universe (there are other universes according to *The Urantia Book,* and the scientists of today are on the verge of proving it) spending a day in the hills with a youth. This event forever exemplifies the willingness of the creator of our universe to fellowship with his creation. This shows we can be alone with Jesus in our own hills or higher mind.

Early Home Life

In the course of this days visiting with John Mark, Jesus spent considerable time comparing their early childhood and later boyhood experiences. Although John's parents possessed more of this world's goods than had Jesus' parents, there was much experience in their boyhood which was very similar. Jesus said many things which helped John better to understand his parents and other members of his family. When the lad asked the Master how he could know that he would turn out to be a "mighty messenger of the kingdom," Jesus said:

"I know you will prove loyal to the gospel of the kingdom because I can depend upon your present faith and love when these qualities are grounded upon such an early training as has been your portion at home. You are the product of a home where the parents bear each other a sincere affection, and therefore you have not been overloved so as injuriously to exalt your concept of self-importance. Neither has your personality suffered distortion in consequence of your parents' loveless maneuvering for your confidence and loyalty, the one against the other. You have enjoyed that parental love which insures laudable self-confidence and which fosters normal feelings of security. But you have also been fortunate in that your parents possessed wisdom as well as love; and it was wisdom which led them to withhold most forms of indulgence and many luxuries which wealth can buy while they sent you to the synagogue school along with your neighborhood playfellows, and they also encouraged you to learn how to live in this world by permitting you to have original experience. You came over to the Jordan, where we preached and John's disciples baptized, with your young friend Amos. Both of you desired to go with us. When you returned to Jerusalem, your parents consented; Amos's parents refused; they loved their son so much that they denied him the blessed experience which you have had, even such as you this day enjoy. By running away from home, Amos could have joined us, but in so doing, he would have wounded love and sacrificed loyalty. Even if such a course had been wise, it would have been a terrible price to pay for experience, independence, and liberty. Wise parents, such as yours, see to it that their children do not have to wound love or stifle loyalty in order to develop independence and enjoy invigorating liberty when they have grown up to your age.

"Love, John, is the supreme reality of the universe when bestowed by all-wise beings, but it is a dangerous and oftentimes semi-selfish trait as it is manifested in the experience of mortal parents. When you get married and have children of your own to rear, make sure that your love is admonished by wisdom and guided by intelligence.

"Your young friend Amos believes this gospel of the kingdom just as much as you, but I cannot fully depend upon him; I am not certain about what he will do in the years to come. His early home life was not such as would produce a wholly dependable person. Amos is too much like one of the apostles who failed to enjoy a normal, loving, and wise home training. Your whole afterlife will be more happy and dependable because you spent your first eight years in a normal and well-regulated home. You possess a strong and well-knit character because you grew up in a home where love prevailed and wisdom reigned. Such childhood training produces a type of loyalty which assures me that you will go through with the course you have begun." [2] I believe this is the John that wrote Revelation and who lived 90 odd years.

The apostles spent most of their day walking about Mount Olivet visiting with disciples who were champing with them. Early in the afternoon, they became anxious to see Jesus as they were concerned about his safety; they felt very lonely without him. There was much talk throughout the day as to whether or not Jesus should have been allowed to go off into the hills with just a young boy. Although no one said anything out loud, all but Judas wished they were in John Mark's place.

It was around mid-afternoon when Nathaniel made a speech on "Supreme Desire" to about half of the apostles and many disciples. At the end of his speech, he was talking about what was wrong with most of us: we are halfhearted; *"We don't love the Master as much as he loves us. If we all wanted to go with him as much as John Mark did, he would have taken us. We stood around while the young lad offered the Master a basket of food and water. When the Master took hold of the basket, the lad wouldn't let go. And so the Master left us here while he went off into the hills with the young lad."*

Around four o'clock that afternoon a runner (messenger that carried news) came to David Zebedee bringing him a message from his mother and Jesus' mother. Several days before that, David had made up his mind; the chief priest and rulers were out to kill Jesus. David was convinced that they would. He was sure Jesus would not use his divine power to save himself, nor would he permit his followers to use force to save him. After reaching these conclusions, he sent a messenger to his mother urging her to come to Jerusalem at once and to bring Jesus' mother and all of his family with her.

David's mother did as she was asked; the runner came back to David and said his mother and Jesus entire family were on their way to Jerusalem. David did all of this on his own; he thought he should keep it to himself; he told no one Jesus' entire family was on their way to Jerusalem.

Judas and the Chief Priest

A short time after Jesus and John Mark left the camp, Judas Iscariot disappeared from the camp not returning until late that afternoon. This confused and discontented Judas went against the Master's request not to go into Jerusalem. He made haste to keep an appointment with Jesus' enemies' at the home of Caiaphas, the Jews high priest. This was an informal meeting that also included the Sanhedrin and was set for 10 o'clock that morning. This meeting was called to discuss the nature of the complaint which should be filed against Jesus and the method to be used to bring him before the Roman authorities for the purpose of getting the necessary civil validation for the death sentence, which they had already passed on Jesus.

The day before, Judas had told some of his relatives and certain Sadducean friends of his father's family that he had reached the conclusion that Jesus was a well meaning dreamer, and he was not the expected messiah of the Jews. Judas told his family and friends that he was trying to find a graceful way to with-draw from the group. His friends convinced him that his withdrawal would be praised by the Jewish rulers as a great event. They made him believe he would receive great honors from the Sanhedrin, and he would be able to erase the stains from his association with untaught heathens.

Judas was convinced Jesus and his group would be defeated by the Jewish rulers, and he didn't want to be identified with a movement that was defeated.

Judas entertained the suggestion of one of his relatives that Jesus was a well meaning fanatic, but was probably not really sound of mind. He always seemed to be a strange and misunderstood person.

And now Judas found himself being resentful that Jesus never assigned him to a job of more importance; although he appreciated being the apostolic treasurer, now he began to feel that he was not appreciated. He found himself overcome with anger towards Peter, James and John because of their closeness to Jesus; he was jealous. Now, on the way to the high priest's home, it was his opportunity to get even with Peter, James and John, more so than being concerned with the thought of betraying Jesus. Right then, a new thought came to the forefront of his mind; he could get even with those that had contributed to the greatest disappointment of his life all the better. So it must be plain to everyone it was not for money that Judas was on his way to Caiaphas, the high priest's home, to arrange for Jesus betrayal; it was revenge.

As he reached the home of Caiaphas, Judas arrived at his final decision to withdraw from Jesus and his fellow apostles. And so having made up his mind to desert the cause of the Kingdom of Heaven, he was determined to grain for himself as much as possible of that honor and glory he thought he'd have when he joined up with Jesus and his fellow apostles. All of the apostles once shared this ambition with Judas, but as time went by, they learned to love truth and love Jesus, at least more than Judas did.

The betrayer was introduced to Caiaphas and the Jewish rulers by his cousin, who explained that Judas had discovered his mistake of allowing himself to be misguided by the subtle teachings of Jesus, and he had reached the decision that he wished to make public the announcement of this mistake and the renunciation of any connection with the Galilean. He asked for his reinstatement in the confidence and fellowship of his Judean Brethrens. Judas' cousin went on to say that Judas felt it would be best if Jesus was taken into custody for the peace of Israel. And as evidence of his sorry for the mistake he had made in participating with such a group, he offered his service to the Sanhedrin in arresting Jesus peacefully. When his cousin finished speaking, he presented Judas. Stepping up to the high priest, Judas told them, *"All that my cousin promised, I will do."* And he asked, *"But what are you willing to give me for my service."* Judas didn't seem to notice a look of contempt come over the face of the high and mighty vainglorious Caiaphas; his heart was too set on self-glory and craving for self-satisfaction.

Caiaphas, looking down on the betrayer told Judas to go with the captain of the guard and arrange with this officer to bring in Jesus that night or tomorrow night. *"And when he is delivered by you into our hands, then you will receive your reward."*

Judas left the home of the high priest and went with the captain of the temple guard to discuss Jesus' apprehension. Judas knew Jesus left camp early that day and had no idea when he would be back, so they arranged to arrest Jesus that following night.

The Real Jesus

Judas returned to the camp of Jesus late that afternoon, overjoyed with thoughts of grandeur and glory that he hadn't had in many days. He realized that there would be no kingdom of heaven as he had conceived it.

Judas didn't realize it at the time, but he was an unconscious critic of Jesus ever since John the Baptist was beheaded by Herod. Judas always resented the fact that Jesus didn't save John. Judas had been a follower of John before joining up with Jesus. He was now saturated with jealousy and overcame with resentment.

Being that it was Wednesday, that evening at camp was a social hour. The Master tried to cheer-up his downhearted apostles. But that was just about impossible. They were beginning to sense something awful was impending. They could not be cheerful, even when Jesus recalled their eventful and loving experiences. Jesus asked about each of the apostles' families. Looking over at David Zebedee, he asked if anyone heard from his mother and family recently. David looked down at his feet for he was afraid to answer.

Even Jesus' cheerfulness and unusual sociability frightened the apostles. They all had a sense that something terrible was just ahead and none felt prepared to face the test. Jesus had been away all day and they had missed him greatly. This Wednesday evening was the lowest of their spiritual status up to the actual hour of the Master's death. The next day was one more day closer to that awful Friday; still, he was with them and they passed through the hour more gracefully.

It was a little before midnight; Jesus, knowing this would be the last night he would sleep through with his chosen family on earth told them to go and rest, *"For tomorrow is one more day of doing the Father will, and the joy of knowing we are his son."*

Jesus had planned on spending this Thursday, his last free day on earth as a divine Son incarnated in the flesh, with his apostles and a few of his devoted disciples. On this beautiful morning, soon after breakfast, Jesus led them to a secluded place a short distance from their camp and he taught them many new truths. The twelve were all present except for Judas. Peter and several of the others mentioned his absence; they assumed Jesus had sent him into the city to prepare for the celebration of the Passover. But Judas did not return to the camp until mid-afternoon, a short time before Jesus had led the twelve into Jerusalem for the Last Supper. At this gathering, among other things, Jesus said to the group:

"This gospel of the kingdom is a living truth. I have told you it is like the leaven in the dough, like the grain of mustard seed; and now I declare that it is like the seed of the living being, which, from generation to generation, while it remains the same living seed, unfailingly unfolds itself in new manifestations and grows acceptably in channels of new adaptation to the peculiar needs and conditions of each successive generation. The revelation I have made to you is a living revelation, and I desire that it shall bear appropriate fruits in each individual and in each generation in accordance with the laws of spiritual growth, increase, and adaptative development. From generation to generation this gospel must show increasing vitality and exhibit greater depth of spiritual power. It must not be permitted to become merely a sacred memory, a mere tradition about me and the times in which we now live. "[3]

Jesus was saying that our religion has to evolve just as everything else in life. We can't keep hanging onto that old time religion and expect to move forward. Over and over, you hear people crying out. "Help me Lord." But their vibration prevents it; they are not making contact. When Jesus concluded his teachings it was about one o'clock in the afternoon. When they got back, David and his group had lunch ready for them.

The Real Jesus

After the Noontime Meal

"Not many of the Master's hearers were able to take in even a part of his forenoon address. Of all who heard him, the Greeks comprehended most. Even the eleven apostles were bewildered by his allusions to future political kingdoms and to successive generations of kingdom believers. Jesus' most devoted followers could not reconcile the impending end of his earthly ministry with these references to an extended future of gospel activities. Some of these Jewish believers were beginning to sense that earth's greatest tragedy was about to take place, but they could not reconcile such an impending disaster with either the Master's cheerfully indifferent personal attitude or his forenoon discourse, wherein he repeatedly alluded to the future transactions of the heavenly kingdom, extending over vast stretches of time and embracing relations with many and successive temporal kingdoms on earth."[4]

By the noontime meal, David Zebedee, through the work of his secret agent in Jerusalem, was fully advised concerning the arrest and killing of Jesus. David was aware of the part Judas had played in the scheme, but never disclosed this knowledge to any of the apostles or disciples. Shortly after lunch he did lead Jesus aside and asked Jesus if he knew—but he never got any further, because Jesus stopped him, saying: *"Yes, David, I know all about it, and I know that you know, but see to it that you tell no man. Only doubt not in your own heart that the will of God will prevail in the end."*

This conversation with David was interrupted by the arrival of a messenger from Philadelphia bringing word that Abner (Abner was a disciple of Jesus working out of Philadelphia) *had heard of the plot to kill Jesus and asking if he should depart for Jerusalem. This runner hastened off for Philadelphia with this word for Abner: "Go on with your work. If I depart from you in the flesh, it is only that I may*

125

return in the spirit. I will not forsake you. I will be with you to the end.[5]

About this time Philip (one of Jesus' Apostles), approached Jesus and mentioned to him that the Passover was drawing near. *"Where you would have us prepare for it?"* When Jesus heard Philip question he answered: *"Go and bring Peter and John, and I will give you direction concerning the supper we will eat together this night; as for the Passover, that you will have to consider after we have first done this."* [6]

Judas saw Philip speaking about these things to Jesus; he tried to get closer, so he could hear their conversation. But David Zebedee, who was standing nearby engaged Judas in a conversation while Peter, John and Philip went to one side to speak with Jesus.

Jesus told them to go right away into Jerusalem, and *"As you enter the gate, you will meet with a man with a water pitcher. He will speak to you and then you should follow him. He would lead you to a certain house, go in after him and asked the man of the house, where is the room that the Master is to eat supper with his apostles? The householder will then show you a large upper room ready for this service."*

This was the home of John Mark's parents; all of this came about as a result of a conversation between Jesus and John Mark during the afternoon of the proceeding day when they were alone in the hills. Jesus wanted to be sure he would have his last supper undisturbed with his apostles. He didn't want Judas to know beforehand of their meeting place; he was afraid Judas would tell his enemies to take him while they were having their last meal. In this way Judas did not learn of their place of meeting until later in the company of Jesus and the other apostles.

It was about four thirty, when the three apostles returned and told Jesus that everything was ready for the supper. Right away, Jesus prepared to lead his twelve apostles over the trail to Bethany Road and on into Jerusalem; this was the last journey he ever made with all twelve of them.

On the Way to the Last Supper

After they were on the road for awhile, Jesus said to the twelve:

"Sit down and rest yourselves while I talk with you about what must shortly come to pass. All these years have I lived with you as brethren, and I have taught you the truth concerning the kingdom of heaven and have revealed to you the mysteries thereof. And my Father has indeed done many wonderful works in connection with my mission on earth. You have been witnesses of all this and partakers in the experience of being laborers together with God. And you will bear me witness that I have for some time warned you that I must presently return to the work the Father has given me to do; I have plainly told you that I must leave you in the world to carry on the work of the kingdom. It was for this purpose that I set you apart, in the hills of Capernaum. The experience you have had with me, you must now make ready to share with others. As the Father sent me into this world, so am I about to send you forth to represent me and finish the work I have begun."[7]

Beginning the Supper

After receiving a warm welcome from John Mark's parents into their home, the apostles went directly to the room they were to eat their supper and Jesus linger behind to talk to the Mark family.

It had been understood beforehand that Jesus wanted to celebrate this time alone with his apostles, so there were no servants provided to wait upon them.

John Mark escorted the apostles to a large room; it was completely furnished for the supper and they saw everything was ready. This long table was surround by thirteen reclining couches just as though it was the celebration of the Passover in a well to do Jewish home.

As the twelve entered the room, they noticed just inside the door, a pitcher, basin and towels for washing their dusty feet; and since there was no servant provided to render this service, the apostles began to look at each other soon as John Mark left the room. They thought to themselves, who's going to wash our feet? No one wanted to act as a servant.

As they stood debating in their hearts, they looked over the setting arrangements of the table; they noticed the higher couch of the host, with one couch on the right and eleven arranged around the table on up to the second seat of honor on the host's right.

They expected any moment for Jesus to walk in, as they stood in a state of uncertainty, whether to sit down or wait for Jesus to assign them their seats. As they hesitated, Judas stepped over to the left seat of honor and indicated he was setting there as the preferred guest. This started up a heated dispute among the other apostles. John Zebedee claimed the other seat of honor on the right. Simon Peter was so irritated at Judas and John Zebedee for assuming they had the rights to those choice positions. As the other angry apostles looked on, he marched around the table and took his place on the lowest couch at the end of the seating order. Since the others had taken the choice seat, Peter figured he take the lowest seat, and hoped when Jesus came and sew him in the lowest seat, he would perhaps give him one of the seats of honor. (All this just goes to show the apostles were humans also).

The apostles were all engaged in voicing their annoyance when Jesus appeared in the doorway, he stood for a moment and a look of disappointment appeared on his face.

They were now ready to eat their supper except their feet had not been washed, and they were not in a good frame of mind. When Jesus walked into the room, they were still making uncomplimentary remarks about each other. You would think those who had been with Jesus for so many years would refrain from publicly expressing their feelings.

For a few minutes after Jesus had taken his seat not a word was spoken. He looked them all over and finally relieving the tension with a smile said: *"I have greatly desired to eat this Passover with you. I wanted to eat with you once more before I suffered, and realizing that my hour has come, I arranged to have this supper with you tonight, for, as concerns the morrow, we are all in the hands of the Father, whose will I have come to execute. I shall not again eat with you until you sit down with me in the kingdom which my Father will give me when I have finished that for which he sent me into this world."*[8]

After the wine and water had been mixed, and Jesus received it from Thaddeus, he held it while he offered thanks, and when he finished, he said: *"Take this cup and divide it among yourselves and, when you partake of it, realize that I shall not again drink with you the fruit of the vine since this is our last supper. When we sit down again in this manner, it will be in the kingdom to come."*[9]

Jesus began to talk to his apostles because he knew his time had come for him to return to the Father; that his work on earth was almost finished. Jesus knew he had revealed the Father's love on earth and had shown the Father's mercy to mankind. And he had completed that which he had come into the world to do, even receiving all power and authority in heaven and on earth. He also was aware Judas Iscariot had fully made up his mind to deliver him that night into the hands of his enemies. He also realized this traitorous betrayal was the work of Judas, but it pleased , the once prince of this world, Lucifer and Satan. But he feared none of those who sought his spiritual overthrow, no more than he feared those who sought his physical demise. The Master had one concern- that his followers would be safe.

Wash the Apostles Feet

It was a Jewish custom at Passover meal after drinking the first cup, for the host to arise from the table and wash his hands. Later on in the meal, and after the second cup, all the guests rose up and washed their hands. The apostles knew that Jesus never observed these rites of ceremonial hand washing, so they were curious to know what he planned after drinking the first cup. After he had drank the first cup, Jesus rose from the table and went over to the door where the water, pitchers, basins, and towels had been placed. Their curiosity turned into amazement as they saw the Master remove his outer garment and put an apron on and began to pour the water into one of the feet basins. Can you imagine the astonishment of the twelve who so recently refused to watch each other's feet and had unseemly disputes over the position at the table? They watched Jesus walk over to the end of the table to the lowest set of the feast, where Simon Peter sat, and kneeled down to wash Simon's feet. As Jesus knelt, all twelve arose as though they were one man rising to their feet. Even the traitorous Judas forgot his evilness for a moment to arise with his fellow apostles in their expression of surprise, respect and amazement.

Peter stood looking down into the upturned face of his Master. Jesus said nothing; it wasn't necessary for him to speak. Peter loved Jesus; this Galilean fisherman was the first human being who wholeheartedly believed in the divinity of Jesus and to make public confession of his belief.

"After a few moments of this great embarrassment, Peter said, "Master, do you really mean to wash my feet?" And then, looking up into Peter's face, Jesus said: "You may not fully understand what I am about to do, but here after you will know the meaning of all these things." Then Simon Peter, drawing a long breath, said, "Master, you shall never wash my feet!" And each of the apostles nodded their

The Real Jesus

approval of Peter's firm declaration of refusal to allow Jesus thus to humble himself before them."[10]

The dramatic demonstration of this unusual scene even touched the heart of Judas Iscariot; but when his vainglorious intellect passed judgment on the scene, he concluded that this gesture of humility conclusively proved that Jesus would never qualify as the Messiah the deliverer of the Jews and he made no mistake in deserting the Master's cause.

As they all stood there in breathless amazement, Jesus said: "Peter, I declare that, if I do not wash your feet, you will have no part with me in that which I am about to perform." When Peter heard this declaration, coupled with the fact that Jesus continued kneeling there at his feet, he made one of those decisions of blind acquiescence in compliance with the wish of one whom he respected and loved. As it began to dawn on Simon Peter that there was attached to this proposed enactment of service some signification that determined one's future connection with the Master's work, he not only became reconciled to the thought of allowing Jesus to wash his feet but, in his characteristic and impetuous manner, said: "Then, Master, wash not my feet only but also my hands and my head."[11]

Jesus went around the table in silence washing the feet of all twelve of his apostles, not even passing Judas. When he had finished washing the feet of his apostles, he put his outer garment back on and went back to his place as host; after looking over his confused apostles, he said:

"Do you really understand what I have done to you? You call me Master, and you say well, for so I am. If, then, the Master has washed your feet, why was it that you were unwilling to wash one another's feet? What lesson should you learn from this parable in which the Master so willingly does that service which his brethren were unwilling to do for one another? Verily, verily, I say to you: A servant is not greater than his master; neither is one who is sent greater than he who sends him. You have seen the way of service in

my life among you, and blessed are you who will have the gracious courage so to serve. But why are you so slow to learn that the secret of greatness in the spiritual kingdom is not like the methods of power in the material world?[12]

"When I came into this chamber tonight, you were not content proudly to refuse to wash one another's feet, but you must also fall to disputing among yourselves as to who should have the places of honor at my table. Such honors the Pharisees and the children of this world seek, but it should not be so among the ambassadors of the heavenly kingdom. Do you not know that there can be no place of preferment at my table? Do you not understand that I love each of you as I do the others? Do you not know that the place nearest me, as men regard such honors, can mean nothing concerning your standing in the kingdom of heaven? You know that the kings of the gentiles have lordship over their subjects, while those who exercise this authority are sometimes called benefactors. But it shall not be so in the kingdom of heaven. He who would be great among you, let him become as the younger; while he who would be chief, let him become as one who serves. Who is the greater, he who sits at meat, or he who serves? Is it not commonly regarded that he who sits at meat is the greater? But you will observe that I am among you as one who serves. If you are willing to become fellow servants with me in doing the Father's will, in the kingdom to come you shall sit with me in power, still doing the Father's will in future glory."[13]

When Jesus stopped speaking, the Alpheus twins (two of Jesus' apostles who were twins) brought on the bread and wine with the bitter herbs and paste of dried fruits for the next course of the Last Supper.

Last Words to the Betrayer

For awhile the apostle ate in silence, but under Jesus' cheerful demeanor, they soon started a conversation; and

The Real Jesus

before long, the meal was proceeding as though nothing had happened that would interfere with this special occasion. After some time had gone by, in about mid-way of the second course of the meal, Jesus, looking them over, said: *"I have told you how much I desired to have this supper with you, and knowing how the evil forces of darkness have conspired to bring about the death of the Son of Man, I determined to eat this supper with you in this secret chamber and a day in advance of the Passover since I will not be with you by this time tomorrow night. I have repeatedly told you that I must return to the Father. Now has my hour come, but it was not required that one of you should betray me into the hands of my enemies."*

When the twelve heard this, having already been robbed of much of their self-assertiveness and self-confidence by the parable of the feet washing and the Master's subsequent discourse, they began to look at one another while in disconcerted tones they hesitatingly inquired, "Is it I?" And when they had all so inquired, Jesus said: "While it is necessary that I go to the Father, it was not required that one of you should become a traitor to fulfill the Father's will. This is the coming to fruit of the concealed evil in the heart of one who failed to love the truth with his whole soul. How deceitful is the intellectual pride that precedes the spiritual downfall! My friend of many years, who even now eats my bread, will be willing to betray me, even as he now dips his hand with me in the dish."[14]

When Jesus finished speaking the apostles were curious and again asked "Is it I?" After a few minutes, Judas, sitting on the left of Jesus, again asked, "Is it I?"

"When Jesus had thus spoken, leaning over toward Judas, he said: "What you have decided to do, do quickly." And when Judas heard these words, he arose from the table and hastily left the room, going out into the night to do what he had set his mind to accomplish. When the other apostles saw Judas hasten off after Jesus had spoken to him, they

thought he had gone to procure something additional for the supper or to do some other errand for the Master since they supposed he still carried the bag."[15]

Establishing the Remembrance Supper

As they brought Jesus the third cup of wine, the "cup of blessing," he arose from the couch and, taking the cup in his hands, blessed it, saying: "Take this cup, all of you, and drink of it. This shall be the cup of my remembrance. This is the cup of the blessing of a new dispensation of grace and truth. This shall be to you the emblem of the bestowal and ministry of the divine Spirit of Truth. And I will not again drink this cup with you until I drink in new form with you in the Father's eternal kingdom."

The apostles all sensed that something out of the ordinary was transpiring as they drank of this cup of blessing in profound reverence and perfect silence. The old Passover commemorated the emergence of their fathers from a state of racial slavery into individual freedom; now the Master was instituting a new remembrance supper as a symbol of the new dispensation wherein the enslaved individual emerges from the bondage of ceremonialism and selfishness into the spiritual joy of the brotherhood and fellowship of the liberated faith sons of the living God.[16]

In Gethsemane

It was about ten O'clock that Thursday night when Jesus and the eleven left the home of Elijah and Mary Mark on their way back to their Gethsemane camp. Since the day in the hills with Jesus, John Mark made it his business to keep a watchful eye on Him. While Jesus and the apostles were eating in the upper room, John mark got a couple hours sleep which he needed; when he heard them coming downstairs, he got up and followed them to their camp, adjacent to Gethsemane Park. John Mark remained so close to the Master throughout the night and the next day, he was a witness to everything on to the hour of his crucifixion.

As Jesus and the eleven apostles started walking on the path to Gethsemane, they wondered what was taking Judas so long. Then they started talking about Jesus' prediction about one of them betraying him. For the first time, they realized all was not well with Judas. But they didn't make open comments about Judas until they reached the camp and saw that he was not there. They all asked Andrew, the chief apostle, where was Judas; he said he didn't know but he suspected he had deserted them.

The Last Group Prayer

A few moments after arriving at camp, Jesus said to them: "My friends and brethren, my time with you is now very short, and I desire that we draw apart by ourselves while we pray to our Father in heaven for strength to sustain us in this hour and henceforth in all the work we must do in his name."

When Jesus had thus spoken, he led the way a short distance up on Olivet, and in full view of Jerusalem he bade them kneel on a large flat rock in a circle about him as they had done on the day of their ordination; and then, as he stood there in the midst of them glorified in the mellow moonlight, he lifted up his eyes toward heaven and prayed:

"Father, my hour has come; now glorify your Son that the Son may glorify you. I know that you have given me full authority over all living creatures in my realm, and I will give eternal life to all who will become faith sons of God. And this is eternal life, that my creatures should know you as the only true God and Father of all, and that they should believe in him whom you sent into the world. Father, I have exalted you on earth and have accomplished the work which

you gave me to do. I have almost finished my bestowal upon the children of our own creation; there remains only for me to lay down my life in the flesh. And now, O my Father, glorify me with the glory which I had with you before this world was and receive me once more at your right hand.

"I have manifested you to the men whom you chose from the world and gave to me. They are yours — as all life is in your hands — you gave them to me, and I have lived among them, teaching them the way of life, and they have believed. These men are learning that all I have comes from you, and that the life I live in the flesh is to make known my Father to the worlds. The truth which you have given to me I have revealed to them. These, my friends and ambassadors, have sincerely willed to receive your word. I have told them that I came forth from you, that you sent me into this world, and that I am about to return to you. Father, I do pray for these chosen men. And I pray for them not as I would pray for the world, but as for those whom I have chosen out of the world to represent me to the world after I have returned to your work, even as I have represented you in this world during my sojourn in the flesh. These men are mine; you gave them to me; but all things which are mine are ever yours, and all that which was yours you have now caused to be mine. You have been exalted in me, and I now pray that I may be honored in these men. I can no longer be in this world; I am about to return to the work you have given me to do. I must leave these men behind to represent us and our kingdom among men. Father, keep these men faithful as I prepare to yield up my life in the flesh. Help these, my friends, to be one in spirit, even as we are one. As long as I could be with them, I could watch over them and guide them, but now am I about to go away. Be near them, Father, until we can send the new teacher to comfort and strengthen them.

"You gave me twelve men, and I have kept them all save one, the son of revenge, who would not have further fellowship with us. These men are weak and frail, but I know

we can trust them; I have proved them; they love me, even as they reverence you. While they must suffer much for my sake, I desire that they should also be filled with the joy of the assurance of sonship in the heavenly kingdom. I have given these men your word and have taught them the truth. The world may hate them, even as it has hated me, but I do not ask that you take them out of the world, only that you keep them from the evil in the world. Sanctify them in the truth; your word is truth. And as you sent me into this world, even so am I about to send these men into the world. For their sakes I have lived among men and have consecrated my life to your service that I might inspire them to be purified through the truth I have taught them and the love I have revealed to them. I well know, my Father, that there is no need for me to ask you to watch over these brethren after I have gone; I know you love them even as I, but I do this that they may the better realize the Father loves mortal men even as does the Son.

"And now, my Father, I would pray not only for these eleven men but also for all others who now believe, or who may hereafter believe the gospel of the kingdom through the word of their future ministry. I want them all to be one, even as you and I are one. You are in me and I am in you, and I desire that these believers likewise be in us; that both of our spirits indwell them. If my children are one as we are one, and if they love one another as I have loved them, all men will then believe that I came forth from you and be willing to receive the revelation of truth and glory which I have made. The glory which you gave me I have revealed to these believers. As you have lived with me in spirit, so have I lived with them in the flesh. As you have been one with me, so have I been one with them, and so will the new teacher ever be one with them and in them. And all this have I done that my brethren in the flesh may know that the Father loves them even as does the Son, and that you love them even as you love me. Father, work with me to save these believers that

they may presently come to be with me in glory and then go on to join you in the Paradise embrace. Those who serve with me in humiliation, I would have with me in glory so that they may see all you have given into my hands as the eternal harvest of the seed sowing of time in the likeness of mortal flesh. I long to show my earthly brethren the glory I had with you before the founding of this world. This world knows very little of you, righteous Father, but I know you, and I have made you known to these believers, and they will make known your name to other generations. And now I promise them that you will be with them in the world even as you have been with me — even so."[17]

Alone in Gethsemane

After things were still and quiet about the camp, Jesus taking Peter, James and John, went a short ways up a nearby gorge where he had often gone and communed with God. The three apostles couldn't help but recognizing that Jesus was very oppressed' they had never seen him so depressed. When they arrived at the place Jesus liked to pray, he told the three to sit down and watch with him while he walked off about a stone's throw to pray: and as he had fallen down on his face, he prayed: *"My Father, I came into this world to do your will, and so have I. I know that the hour has come to lay down this life in the flesh, and I do not shrink therefrom, but I would know that it is your will that I drink this cup. Send me the assurance that I will please you in my death even as I have in my life."[18]*

Jesus remained in prayer for a few moments, then going to the three apostles, he found they were sound asleep; their eyes were heavy and they could not remain awake. As Jesus awoke them, he said: *"What! can you not watch with me even for one hour? Cannot you see that my soul is exceedingly sorrowful, even to death, and that I crave your companionship?"* After the three had aroused from their *slumber, the Master again went apart by himself and, falling down on the ground, again prayed: "Father, I know it is possible to avoid this cup — all things are possible with you — but I have come to do your will, and while this is a bitter cup, I would drink it if it is your will." And when he had thus prayed, a mighty angel came down by his side and, speaking to him, touched him and strengthened him.*

When Jesus returned to speak with the three apostles, he again found them fast asleep. He awakened them, saying: "In such an hour I need that you should watch and pray with me — all the more do you need to pray that you enter not into temptation — wherefore do you fall asleep when I leave you?"

And then, for a third time, the Master withdrew and prayed: "Father, you see my sleeping apostles; have mercy upon them. The spirit is indeed willing, but the flesh is weak. And now, O Father, if this cup may not pass, then would I drink it. Not my will, but yours, be done." And when he had finished praying, he lay for a moment prostrate on the ground. When he arose and went back to his apostles, once more he found them asleep. He surveyed them and, with a pitying gesture, tenderly said: "Sleep on now and take your rest; the time of decision is past. The hour is now upon us wherein the Son of Man will be betrayed into the hands of his enemies." As he reached down to shake them that he might awaken them, he said: "Arise, let us be going back to the camp, for, behold, he who betrays me is at hand, and the hour has come when my flock shall be scattered. But I have already told you about these things."[19]

The Betrayer and the Arrest of Jesus

After Jesus had finally awakened Peter, James and John, he suggested they go to their tents and get some sleep, so that they will be ready for the next day duties. But now the three were wide awake because they were rested from their short naps. Beside they were excited by the two messengers that had entered the camp and asked for David Zebedee, and went right away to the area where Peter had told them he was keeping watch.

Although the eight apostles were sound asleep, the Greeks who were encamped next to them, were so fearful of trouble, they had posted a guard to give the alarm in case of danger. When these two messengers entered the camp, the Greek guard went and woke up all of his countrymen who ran from their tents fully dressed and fully armed. All the camp was now up except for the eight apostles. Peter was going to wake them, but Jesus forbade him. Jesus suggested they go to their tents, but they were reluctant to go. Jesus left his followers and walked down to the Olive Press, near the entrance to Gethsemane Park. The three apostles, the Greeks, and others member of the camp followed after him; but John Mark went around another way through olive trees and hid himself in a small shed near the Olive Press.

Jesus left the camp, so that when they came to arrest him, they wouldn't disturb his apostles. He was afraid that if the apostles were awoke at the time of his arrest, seeing Judas betraying him would infuriate the apostles and they would resist the soldiers and be arrested along with him and share his fate.

Jesus knew the plans for his death started with the councils of the rulers of the Jews; he was also aware that all such evil doings had the full approval of Lucifer, Caligastia (the one Jesus called the prince of this world) and Satan. And he also was aware that they wanted to see all of the apostles destroyed with him. So Jesus sat alone on the Olive Press where no one saw him but John Mark and a host of celestial beings.

The Real Jesus

The Father's Will

There is great danger of misunderstanding the meaning of numerous sayings and many events associated with the termination of the Master's career in the flesh. The cruel treatment of Jesus by the ignorant servants and the calloused soldiers, the unfair conduct of his trials, and the unfeeling attitude of the professed religious leaders, must not be confused with the fact that Jesus, in patiently submitting to all this suffering and humiliation, was truly doing the will of the Father in Paradise. It was, indeed and in truth, the will of the Father that his Son should drink to the full the cup of mortal experience, from birth to death, but the Father in heaven had nothing whatever to do with instigating the barbarous behavior of those supposedly civilized human beings who so brutally tortured the Master and so horribly heaped successive indignities upon his nonresisting person. These inhuman and shocking experiences which Jesus was called upon to endure in the final hours of his mortal life were not in any sense a part of the divine will of the Father, which his human nature had so triumphantly pledged to carry out at the time of the final surrender of man to God as signified in the threefold prayer which he indited in the garden while his weary apostles slept the sleep of physical exhaustion.

The Father in heaven desired the bestowal Son to finish his earth career naturally, just as all mortals must finish up their lives on earth and in the flesh. Ordinary men and women cannot expect to have their last hours on earth and the supervening episode of death made easy by a special dispensation. Accordingly, Jesus elected to lay down his life in the flesh in the manner which was in keeping with the outworking of natural events, and he steadfastly refused to extricate himself from the cruel clutches of a wicked conspiracy of inhuman events which swept on with horrible certainty toward his unbelievable humiliation and *ignominious death. And every bit of all this astounding manifestation of hatred and this unprecedented demonstration of cruelty was the work of evil men and wicked mortals. God in heaven did not will it, neither did the archenemies of Jesus dictate it, though they did much to insure that unthinking and evil mortals would thus reject the bestowal Son. Even the father of sin turned his face away from the excruciating horror of the scene of the crucifixion.[20]*

After Judas suddenly left the table while eating the Last Supper, he went directly to the home of his cousin. Then, the two of them went straight to the captain of the temple guards. Judas asked the captain of the guards to get ready his temple guards as he was ready to lead them to Jesus. Judas appeared a little before he was expected, so there was some delay getting started to the Mark home, where Judas expected to find Jesus, and his eleven apostles still visiting. The Master and his apostle left the Mark home fifteen minutes before Judas and the guards had arrived. By the time the betrayer and the guards reached the Mark home, Jesus and the eleven were well outside of the wall of the city and well on their way back to their camp.

Judas was very disturbed at their failure to find Jesus at the Mark home and in the company of the eleven apostles; only two of them were armed for resistance. Judas knew that afternoon when they had left the camp on the way to the Mark's home that only Peter and Simon Zelotes were armed with swords. Judas hoped to take Jesus when the city was quiet, and there was little chance of resistance. He was afraid that if they waited until they returned to their camp, more than sixty devoted disciples would be there, and he also knew Simon Zelotes had quite a few arms stored which he had access to.

Judas was becoming very nervous as he thought about how the other apostles would detest him and he feared they would try to kill him. He was not only disloyal, but also a real coward. When they failed to find Jesus in the upper

The Real Jesus

room, Judas asked the captain of the guard to return to the temple. By this time, the ruler of the Jews had started to gather at the high priest's home to prepare for receiving Jesus. Their bargain with the traitor called for Jesus to be arrested by midnight of that day.

Judas explain to his associates that they had missed Jesus at the Mark home, and it would be necessary for them to go to Gethsemane to arrest him. The betrayer went on to say them there were sixty devoted followers of Jesus at the camp and all were armed. The rulers of the Jews reminded Judas that Jesus always preached nonviolence; Judas replied they could not relay on all of Jesus' followers to go alone with that program. But he really feared for his own hide and asked for a company of forty soldiers. The Jewish authorities did not have such a force under their power, so they went at once to the fortress of Antonia and asked the Roman commander for these soldiers. But when Antonia learned that they intended to arrest Jesus, he refused and referred them to his superior. They finally had to go to Pontius Pilate himself.

It was late when they arrived at Pilate's house; Pilate had retired for the night to his chambers with his wife. At first he hesitated about having anything to do with the arrest of Jesus since his wife had asked him not to grant the request. But since the presiding officer of the Jewish Sanhedrin was present, the governor thought it wise to grant the request.

Judas started out around eleven thirty with about sixty people accompanying him: temple guards, Roman soldiers and curious servants of the chief priest and rulers. And so this group of armed soldiers and guards, carrying torches and lanterns, approached Gethsemane Garden; Judas stepped well in front of the group, so that he could identify Jesus quickly and the apprehenders could quickly arrest him before Jesus followers could rally to his defense. Another reason Judas decided to reach the garden before the solders was because he tried to make it appear that he was ahead of the

143

solders to warn Jesus and the others apostles. But his scheming didn't work; although Jesus greeted Judas with kindness, he greeted him as a traitor.

As soon as Peter, James and John, with about thirty of their campers, saw the armed band with torches and lanterns swing around the bottom of the hill, they knew they were soldiers coming to arrest Jesus; they all ran down to the Olive Press where Jesus was sitting in the moonlight alone. As the company of soldiers approached on one side, the three apostles approached on the other. Judas stepped forward and stood in front of Jesus; the two groups stood motionless. Jesus was in between the two groups, and Judas was getting ready to place the traitorous kiss upon Jesus' brow.

Judas was wishing that he could after leading the soldiers to Gethsemane, point Jesus out to the soldiers or at most carry out his promise to greet him with a kiss, then quickly leave the scene. Judas was afraid all of the apostles would be present and attack him for betraying their beloved teacher. But when the Master Jesus greeted him as a traitor, it so confused him, he made no attempt to flee.

Jesus made one last effort to save Judas before the traitor actually betrayed him; before Judas could reach him, Jesus called out to the soldiers on his left saying to the captain, "Whom do you seek?" The captain answered, "Jesus of Nazareth." Stepping in front of the captain, standing there in majestic splendor of the God of this creation, Jesus said "I am he."[21] Many of these soldiers and guards had heard Jesus teach in the temple; other had heard about his great works. And when they heard him so bravely announce his identity, those in the front rank fell suddenly backward. They were awed with surprise at his clam and splendid announcement of his identity. There was no need for Judas to carry out his betrayal. Jesus had boldly presented himself to his enemies, and they could take him without Judas' help. But the traitor had to account for his presence there and besides, he wanted to keep his bargain with the rulers of the Jews. He wanted to receive his great reward and the honor he thought would be given to him in payment for his promise to deliver Jesus into their hands.

As the soldiers regrouped themselves from the powerful impression of Jesus' presence and the sound of his unusual voice, Judas walked up to Jesus, and placing a kiss upon his brow, said: *"Hail Master and teacher." And as Judas hugged the Master, Jesus said: "Friend, is it enough to do this? Would you even betray the Son of Man with a kiss.?"*[22]

The apostles and disciples were literally shocked at what they had seen. For a while, no one moved. Then Jesus pushed himself free from the traitor's grip and stepped up to the guards and soldiers and again asked: *"Who do you seek?"* and again the captain said: *Jesus of Nazareth."* And he again answered: *"I have told you that I am he. If therefore, you seek me, let these other go their way. I am ready to go with you."*[23] The captain was willing to let the three apostles and their associates go their way in peace.

But before they started, as Jesus stood there waiting for the captain's orders, one of the bodyguards of the high priest named Malchus, stepped up to Jesus and was ready to bind Jesus' hands behind him; the Roman captain had told no one to bind Jesus. When Peter and the rest of Jesus' followers saw their Master being subjected to such humiliation, they were no longer able to restrain themselves. Peter drew his sword and with the others, rushed forward to strike Malchus. But before the soldiers could come to the defense of the high priest servant, Jesus raised a forbidding hand and speaking sternly, said: "Peter, put up your sword. *They who take the sword shall perish by the sword. Do you not understand that it is the Father's will that I drink this cup? And do you not further know that I could even now command more than twelve legions of angels and their associates, who would deliver me from the hands of these few men?"*[24]

Jesus put a stop to the physical resistance by his followers; their display of resistance aroused the fear of the captain of the soldiers who by now with help, quickly bound Jesus.

After Jesus had been bound, the captain, fearing Jesus' followers would try to rescue him, gave orders that they be seized; but the soldiers were not quick enough. Peter and his associates overheard the captain's orders to arrest them, and they quickly ran back into the gorge. All this, time John Mark remained hidden in the nearby shed. When the guards started back to Jerusalem with Jesus, John Mark attempted to sneak out of the shed to catch up with the apostles and disciples. But just as he came out of the shed, one of the last returning soldiers who had run after the disciples, saw him coming out of the shed and started chasing him.

As a matter of fact, the soldier got close enough to grab Mark's coat, but the young man freed himself by getting out of the coat running naked while the solder held the empty coat. John Mark caught up with David Zebedee on the upper trail. When he finished telling all that had happened, they both hurried back to the tents of the sleeping apostles and informed all of the Master's betrayal and arrest. At about the same time the eight apostles were being awakened, those who had fled up the ravine, were returning. They all gathered by the Olive Press to discuss what could be done about Jesus' arrest. (They were all confused as it was difficult for them to believe this was happening). While this was going on, Peter and John Zebedee who had hidden among the olive trees, had already gone on after the soldiers and guards who were now leading Jesus back to Jerusalem as though he were a dangerous criminal. John followed close behind the group, but Peter kept his distance.

After John Mark escaped from the soldiers, he went into Peter and John Zebedee's tent and found himself a coat. He suspected they would take Jesus to the home of Annas the former high priest; so he edged around the Olive Orchard and was there ahead of the soldiers hiding near the entrance to the gate of the high priest's palace.

On the Way to the High Priest Palace

Before they left the garden with Jesus, a dispute broke out between the captain of the Jewish guard and the captain of the Roman soldiers as to where they were to take Jesus. The captain of the temple guard gave orders that he should be taken to Caiaphas, the acting high priest. The captain of the Roman soldiers gave orders that Jesus should be taken to the palace of Annas, the former high priest and father-in-law of Caiaphas. And this they did because the Romans were used to dealing with Annas in all things that dealt with the enforcement of the Jewish ecclesiastical laws. The orders of the Roman captain were obeyed; they took Jesus to the home of Annas for basic examination. Judas marched alongside the captains hearing everything that was said, but took no part in the dispute; neither the Jewish captain or the Roman captain would not as much as speak to the betrayer as they held him in such contempt.

At about this time, John Zebedee recalled the Master once telling him to remain always near at hand and he hurried up to be near Jesus as he marched along between the two captains. The commander of the temple guard saw him come up alongside and told his assistant to arrest John, that he was one of this fellow's followers. But when the Roman captain heard this, he looked up and saw John; he gave orders that the apostle should come over by him. Then the Roman captain said to the Jewish captain, *"This man is neither a traitor nor a coward. I saw him in the garden and he did not draw a sword to resist us. He has the courage to come forth to be with his Master and no man shall lay upon him."*

The Roman law allows that any prisoner may have at least one friend to stand with him before the judgment bar and this man will not be prevented from standing by the side of his Master, the prisoner. The Jews were afraid to say anything to John or to harm him in anyway, because he had somewhat of a status of a Roman counselor selected to act as an observer of the transactions of the Jewish ecclesiastical court. (This explains why John Zebedee was allowed to be with Jesus throughout this hold ordeal). When Judas heard this, he was so humiliated and ashamed, he dropped back behind the group coming up to the palace of Annas. John's situation was made even more secure when, turning Jesus over to the captain of the temple guards at the gate of Anna's palace, the Roman captain told his assistant to go along with this prisoner and see that the Jews do not kill him without Pilate's consent. And he told his assistant to see that the Galilean was permitted to stand by and observe everything that went on. So John was able to be near Jesus right up to his death on the cross, while the other ten apostles remained in hiding.

All the way to the palace of Annas, Jesus didn't say a word. From the time of his arrest to the time of his appearance before Annas, Jesus said nothing.

Examination by Annas

Men appointed by Annas had secretly instructed the captain of the Roman soldiers to take Jesus right away to the palace of Annas after his arrest. The former high priest wanted to keep up his prestige as chief ecclesiastical authority of the Jews. The other reason Annas wanted to keep Jesus at his house for several hours was to allow time to legally call the court of the Sanhedrin it was not lawful to convene the Sanhedrin court before the time of the offering of the morning sacrifice in the temple, and the sacrifice was offered around three o'clock in the morning.

Annas knew that a court was in waiting at the palace of his son-in-law, Caiaphas. There were thirty members of the

Sanhedrin court gathered at the home of the high priest, so they'd be ready to sit in judgment of Jesus when he was brought before them.

Annas, made rich by the temple revenues, his son-in-law, the acting high priest, and his relationship with the Roman authority, was the most powerful, single person in all Jewry.

"Annas had not seen Jesus for several years, not since the time when the Master called at his house and immediately left upon observing his coldness and reserve in receiving him. Annas had thought to presume on this early acquaintance and thereby attempt to persuade Jesus to abandon his claims and leave Palestine. He was reluctant to participate in the murder of a good man and had reasoned that Jesus might choose to leave the country rather than to suffer death. But when Annas stood before the stalwart and determined Galilean, he knew at once that it would be useless to make such proposals. Jesus was even more majestic and well poised than Annas remembered him.

When Jesus was young, Annas had taken a great interest in him, but now his revenues were threatened by what Jesus had so recently done in driving the money-changers and other commercial traders out of the temple. This act had aroused the enmity of the former high priest far more than had Jesus' teachings.

Annas entered his spacious audience chamber, seated himself in a large chair, and commanded that Jesus be brought before him. After a few moments spent in silently surveying the Master, he said: "You realize that something must be done about your teaching since you are disturbing the peace and order of our country." As Annas looked inquiringly at Jesus, the Master looked full into his eyes but made no reply. Again Annas spoke, "What are the names of your disciples, besides Simon Zelotes, the agitator?" Again Jesus looked down upon him, but he did not answer.

Annas was considerably disturbed by Jesus' refusal to answer his questions, so much so that he said to him: "Do you have no care as to whether I am friendly to you or not? Do you have no regard for the power I have in determining the issues of your coming trial?" When Jesus heard this, he said: "Annas, you know that you could have no power over me unless it were permitted by my Father. Some would destroy the Son of Man because they are ignorant; they know no better, but you, friend, know what you are doing. How can you, therefore, reject the light of God?"

The kindly manner in which Jesus spoke to Annas almost bewildered him. But he had already determined in his mind that Jesus must either leave Palestine or die; so he summoned up his courage and asked: "Just what is it you are trying to teach the people? What do you claim to be?" Jesus answered: "You know full well that I have spoken openly to the world. I have taught in the synagogues and many times in the temple, where all the Jews and many of the gentiles have heard me. In secret I have spoken nothing; why, then, do you ask me about my teaching? Why do you not summon those who have heard me and inquire of them? Behold, all Jerusalem has heard that which I have spoken even if you have not yourself heard these teachings." But before Annas could make reply, the chief steward of the palace, who was standing near, struck Jesus in the face with his hand, saying, "How dare you answer the high priest with such words?" Annas spoke no words of rebuke to his steward, but Jesus addressed him, saying, "My friend, if I have spoken evil, bear witness against the evil; but if I have spoken the truth, why, then, should you smite me?"

Although Annas regretted that his steward had struck Jesus, he was too proud to take notice of the matter. In his confusion he went into another room, leaving Jesus alone with the household attendants and the temple guards for almost an hour.

The Real Jesus

When he returned, going up to the Master's side, he said, "Do you claim to be the Messiah, the deliverer of Israel?" Said Jesus: "Annas, you have known me from the times of my youth. You know that I claim to be nothing except that which my Father has appointed, and that I have been sent to all men, gentile as well as Jew." Then said Annas: "I have been told that you have claimed to be the Messiah; is that true?" Jesus looked upon Annas but only replied, "So you have said."

About this time messengers arrived from the palace of Caiaphas to inquire what time Jesus would be brought before the court of the Sanhedrin, and since it was nearing the break of day,· Annas thought best to send Jesus bound and in the custody of the temple guards to Caiaphas. He himself followed after them shortly."[25]

I wonder what would our lives in the Western World be like today if Jesus had decided to leave Palestine? But Jesus was determined to do God's will by dying to prove to us that life is a continuum, although it will be in another dimension; Jesus told us in John 18:36, *"My kingdom is not of this world."* He was trying to teach that there are other worlds.

Peter in the Courtyard

As the group of soldiers and guards came to the entrance of the palace of Annas, John Zebedee was marching by the side of the captain of the Roman soldiers. Judas had dropped some distance behind and Simon Peter even farther back. After John had reached the palace courtyard with Jesus and the guards, Judas came up to the gate, but after seeing John and Jesus, Judas went over to the home of Caiaphas where he knew the real trial of Jesus was to take place.

Soon after Judas left, Simon Peter arrived; as he stood by the gate, John noticed him just as they were getting ready to take Jesus into the palace. The gate keeper knew John, and when he spoke to her to let Peter in, she gladly obliged. After he entered the courtyard, Peter went over were they had a charcoal fire to warm himself as the night was chilly. Peter felt out of place among the enemies of Jesus. And he was out of place. Jesus had not told him to keep close at hand as he did John. Peter should have been with the other apostles, who had been warned not to endanger their lives during the trial and crucifixion of Jesus. Peter had throw away his sword a short time before reaching the place gate. He was extremely confused; he could not believe Jesus was arrested; he had a difficult time grasping the reality of the situation, that he was there in the courtyard of Annas the high priest warming himself amongst the servants of the high priest. He wondered what the other apostles were doing.

Shortly after the gate guard let Peter in, and while he was warming himself near the fire, she went over to him and asked if he wasn't one of that man's disciples? Peter thought of saving himself and quickly denied that he was. Doing the next couple of hours, two more people asked him the same question and he vehemently denied knowing Jesus. The third time he denied the accusation, the cock crowed; then Peter remembered the words of the Master earlier that night that he would deny him three times before the cock crowed. As he stood there feeling guilty, the palace doors opened and the guard led Jesus past on the way to Caiaphas. As Jesus passed by Peter, he saw by the light of the torches, a look of despair on the face of his former self-confident and brave apostle; and he turned and look upon Peter. Peter never forgot that look as long as he lived. It was such a glance of pity and love that mortal man had ever seen on the face of Jesus.

After Jesus and the guard left the palace gate, Peter followed them for a while, but he could not go any farther. He sat down by the side of the road and what seemed to be a river of water ran from his eyes. After he had shed the tears of anguish, he went back toward the camp, hoping to find his brother Andrew. When he reached the camp, he found only

Before the Sanhedrin Court

David Zebedee who sent a massager with Peter to show him where his brother was hiding in Jerusalem.

Before the Sanhedrin Court

It was three thirty that Friday morning when the chief priest, Caiaphas, brought the Sanhedrin court of inquiry into session and asked that Jesus be brought in for the proceedings. On three different occasions, the Sanhedrin by a large majority vote had already sentenced Jesus to death. They decided he was worthy of informal charges of lawbreaking, blasphemy and showing contempt for the laws of Israel.

Usually, the Jews, when trying a man on capital charges, proceeded with great caution and provided every safeguard of fairness in the selection of witnesses and the entire conduct of the trial. On this particular occasion, though Caiaphas was more of a prosecutor than an unbiased Judge.

Jesus appeared before the court clothed in his usual garments and his hands tied behind his back. The entire court were surprised and confused by his majestic appearance. Never had they looked upon such a prisoner nor saw such composure in a man on trial for his life. I will quote the remainder of this section for the benefit of the reader.

"The Jewish law required that at least two witnesses must agree upon any point before a charge could be laid against the prisoner. Judas could not be used as a witness against Jesus because the Jewish law specifically forbade the testimony of a traitor. More than a score of false witnesses were on hand to testify against Jesus, but their testimony was so contradictory and so evidently trumped up that the Sanhedrims themselves were very much ashamed of the performance. Jesus stood there, looking down benignly upon these perjurers, and his very countenance disconcerted the lying witnesses. Throughout all this false testimony, the

Master never said a word; he made no reply to their many false accusations.

The first time any two of their witnesses approached even the semblance of an agreement was when two men testified that they had heard Jesus say in the course of one of his temple discourses that he would "destroy this temple made with hands and in three days make another temple without hands." That was not exactly what Jesus said, regardless of the fact that he pointed to his own body when he made the remark referred to.

Although the high priest shouted at Jesus, "Do you not answer any of these charges?" Jesus opened not his mouth. He stood there in silence while all of these false witnesses gave their testimony. Hatred, fanaticism, and unscrupulous exaggeration so characterized the words of these perjurers that their testimony fell in its own entanglements. The very best refutation of their false accusations was the Master's calm and majestic silence.

Shortly after the beginning of the testimony of the false witnesses, Annas arrived and took his seat beside Caiaphas. Annas now arose and argued that this threat of Jesus to destroy the temple was sufficient to warrant three charges against him:

1. That he was a dangerous traducer of the people. That he taught them impossible things and otherwise deceived them.

2. That he was a fanatical revolutionist in that he advocated laying violent hands on the sacred temple, else how could he destroy it?

3. That he taught magic inasmuch as he promised to build a new temple, and that without hands.

Already had the full Sanhedrin agreed that Jesus was guilty of death-deserving transgressions of the Jewish laws, but they were now more concerned with developing charges regarding his conduct and teachings which would justify Pilate in pronouncing the death sentence upon their prisoner. They knew that they must secure the consent of the Roman governor before Jesus could legally be put to death. And Annas was minded to proceed along the line of making it appear that Jesus was a dangerous teacher to be abroad among the people.

But Caiaphas could no longer endure the sight of the Master standing there in perfect composure and unbroken silence. He thought he knew at least one way in which the prisoner might be induced to speak. Accordingly, he rushed over to the side of Jesus and, shaking his accusing finger in the Master's face, said: "I adjure you, in the name of the living God, that you tell us whether you are the Deliverer, the Son of God." Jesus answered Caiaphas: "I am. Soon I go to the Father, and presently shall the Son of Man be clothed with power and once more reign over the hosts of heaven."

When the high priest heard Jesus utter these words, he was exceedingly angry, and rending his outer garments, he exclaimed: "What further need have we of witnesses? Behold, now have you all heard this man's blasphemy. What do you now think should be done with this lawbreaker and blasphemer?" And they all answered in unison, "He is worthy of death; let him be crucified."

Jesus manifested no interest in any question asked him when before Annas or the Sanhedrims except the one question relative to his bestowal mission. When asked if he were the Son of God, he instantly and unequivocally answered in the affirmative.

Annas desired that the trial proceed further, and that charges of a definite nature regarding Jesus' relation to the Roman law and Roman institutions be formulated for subsequent presentation to Pilate. The councilors were anxious to carry these matters to a speedy termination, not only because it was the preparation day for the Passover and no secular work should be done after noon, but also because they feared Pilate might any time return to the Roman capital of Judea, Caesarea, since he was in Jerusalem only for the Passover celebration.

But Annas did not succeed in keeping control of the court. After Jesus had so unexpectedly answered Caiaphas, the high priest stepped forward and smote him in the face with his hand. Annas was truly shocked as the other members of the court, in passing out of the room, spit in Jesus' face, and many of them mockingly slapped him with the palms of their hands. And thus in disorder and with such unheard of confusion this first session of the Sanhedrims trial of Jesus ended at half past four o'clock.

Thirty prejudiced and tradition-blinded false judges, with their false witnesses, are presuming to sit in judgment on the righteous Creator of a universe. And these impassioned accusers are exasperated by the majestic silence and superb bearing of this God-man. His silence is terrible to endure; his speech is fearlessly defiant. He is unmoved by their threats and undaunted by their assaults. Man sits in judgment on God, but even then he loves them and would save them if he could. "[26]

The Hour of Humiliation

The Jewish law necessitate that in passing of the death sentence, there should be two sessions of the court. The second was to be held on the next day and the time in between was to be spent fasting and mourning by the members of the court. These men could not wait until the next day to confirm their decision that Jesus must die. They waited only one hour. Jesus was left in the audience chamber in the care of the temple guards who, with servants of the high priest, amused themselves by doing all kinds of terrible things to Jesus; they kept striking him in the face with some type of rod, spitting on him and all sorts of indignity. They would strike him in the face with the rod and then asked him to prophesy to them. This went on for a whole hour, mistreating this unresisting man of Galilee.

During this awful hour of suffering and mock trial before these ignorant and non-feeling guards and servants, John Zebedee waited in lonely terror in an adjoining room. When these abuse first started, Jesus indicated to John by nodding his head he should go into another room. Jesus knew that if his apostle stayed in the room to see this abusive treatments, John resentment and protests would probably result in his death.

Second Meeting of the Court

At five thirty that morning, the court reassembled and Jesus was led into the adjoining room where John was waiting. Here, the Roman soldiers and temple guards watched over Jesus while the court began putting together the charges that were to be presented to Pilate.

"This session of the court lasted only a half hour, and when they adjourned to go before Pilate, they had drawn up the indictment of Jesus, as being worthy of death, under three heads:

1. That he was a perverter of the Jewish nation; he deceived the people and incited them to rebellion.

2. That he taught the people to refuse to pay tribute to Caesar.

3. That, by claiming to be a king and the founder of a new sort of kingdom, he incited treason against the emperor.

This entire procedure was irregular and wholly contrary to the Jewish laws. No two witnesses had agreed on any matter except those who testified regarding Jesus' statement about destroying the temple and raising it again in three days. And even concerning that point, no witnesses spoke for the defense, and neither was Jesus asked to explain his intended meaning.

The only point the court could have consistently judged him on was that of blasphemy, and that would have rested entirely on his own testimony. Even concerning blasphemy, they failed to cast a formal ballot for the death sentence.

And now they presumed to formulate three charges, with which to go before Pilate, on which no witnesses had been heard, and which were agreed upon while the accused prisoner was absent. When this was done, three of the Pharisees took their leave; they wanted to see Jesus destroyed, but they would not formulate charges against him without witnesses and in his absence.

Jesus did not again appear before the Sanhedrist court. They did not want again to look upon his face as they sat in judgment upon his innocent life. Jesus did not know (as a man) of their formal charges until he heard them recited by Pilate.

While Jesus was in the room with John and the guards, and while the court was in its second session, some of the women about the high priest's palace, together with their friends, came to look upon the strange prisoner, and one of them asked him, "Are you the Messiah, the Son of God?" And Jesus answered: "If I tell you, you will not believe me; and if I ask you, you will not answer.[27]

A little after six o'clock that morning, April 7, A.D. 30, according to *The Urantia Book,* Jesus was brought to Pilate the Roman procurator who governed Judea, Samaria, and Idumea that was supervised by the governing body of Syria. Jesus was taken in front of the Roman governor by the temple guards, bound, and was followed by about fifty of his accusers and the Sanhedrin court (principally Sadduceans) Iscariot, the high priest, Caiaphas and followed by the apostle John. Annas did not appear before Pilate.

When Jesus and his accusers gathered in front of Pilate's judgment hall, the Roman governor came out and addressing the group that gathered, asked: *"What accusation do you bring against this fellow?"* The Sadducees and

The Real Jesus

councilors had taken it upon themselves to get rid of Jesus and were determined to go before Pilate and ask for the confirmation of the death sentence to be pronounced upon Jesus without stating any definite charges; the spokesman for the Sanhedrist court answered Pilate: *"If this man were not an evildoer, we should not have delivered him up to you."*

When Pilate saw that they were a little leery to state their charges against Jesus, he knew they had been up all night deliberating as to his guilt; he answered them: *"Since you have not agreed on any definite charges, why do you not take this man and pass judgment on him in accordance your own law?"* Then said the clerk of the Sanhedrin court to Pilate: *"It is not lawful for us to put any man to death, and this disturber of our nation is worthy to die for the things he said and done. Therefore have we come before you for confirmation of this decree."* [28]

If their law didn't allow them to kill any man, what about stoning people to death? Here, they got the Romans to do their dirty work. I don't know about their way of thinking, but, to me that seemed to be a greater sin, because they got another soul involved in their wrong doing; they were still responsible for the death of Jesus, even though someone else performed the act.

Pilate knew about Jesus' work among the Jews so he figured the charges brought against Jesus had to do with infringement of the Jewish ecclesiastical laws; so, he referred the case back to their own tribunal. It was a few hours before midnight and after he had granted permission to use Roman soldiers in the secret arrest of Jesus Pilate learned more about Jesus and his teachings from his wife Claudia, who was a partial convert to Judaism, and who later became a full fledged believer in Jesus' gospel.

Pilate wanted to postpone this case, but he saw how the Jewish leaders had their minds made up to go on with the case. He knew that this day was the morning of the Passover and it was Friday, the preparation for the Jewish Sabbath.

The Private Examination by Pilate

"Pilate took Jesus and John Zebedee into a private chamber, leaving the guards outside in the hall, and requesting the prisoner to sit down, he sat down by his side and asked several questions. Pilate began his talk with Jesus by assuring him that he did not believe the first count against him: that he was a perverter of the nation and an inciter to rebellion. Then he asked, "Did you ever teach that tribute should be refused Caesar?" Jesus, pointing to John, said, "Ask him or any other man who has heard my teaching." Then Pilate questioned John about this matter of tribute, and John testified concerning his Master's teaching and explained that Jesus and his apostles paid taxes both to Caesar and to the temple. When Pilate had questioned John, he said, "See that you tell no man that I talked with you." And John never did reveal this matter.

Pilate then turned around to question Jesus further, saying: "And now about the third accusation against you, are you the king of the Jews?" Since there was a tone of possibly sincere inquiry in Pilate's voice, Jesus smiled on the procurator and said: "Pilate, do you ask this for yourself, or do you take this question from these others, my accusers?" Whereupon, in a tone of partial indignation, the governor answered: "Am I a Jew? Your own people and the chief priests delivered you up and asked me to sentence you to death. I question the validity of their charges and am only trying to find out for myself what you have done. Tell me, have you said that you are the king of the Jews, and have you sought to found a new kingdom?"

Then said Jesus to Pilate: "Do you not perceive that my kingdom is not of this world? If my kingdom were of this world, surely would my disciples fight that I should not be delivered into the hands of the Jews. My presence here before you in these bonds is sufficient to show all men that my kingdom is a spiritual dominion, even the brotherhood of men who, through faith and by love, have become the sons of God. And this salvation is for the gentile as well as for the Jew."

"Then you are a king after all?" said Pilate. And Jesus answered: "Yes, I am such a king, and my kingdom is the family of the faith sons of my Father who is in heaven. For this purpose was I born into this world, even that I should show my Father to all men and bear witness to the truth of God. And even now do I declare to you that every one who loves the truth hears my voice."

Then said Pilate, half in ridicule and half in sincerity, "Truth, what is truth — who knows?"

Pilate was not able to fathom Jesus' words, nor was he able to understand the nature of his spiritual kingdom, but he was now certain that the prisoner had done nothing worthy of death. One look at Jesus, face to face, was enough to convince even Pilate that this gentle and weary, but majestic and upright, man was no wild and dangerous revolutionary who aspired to establish himself on the temporal throne of Israel. Pilate thought he understood something of what Jesus meant when he called himself a king, for he was familiar with the teachings of the Stoics, who declared that "the wise man is king." Pilate was thoroughly convinced that, instead of being a dangerous seditionmonger, Jesus was nothing more or less than a harmless visionary, an innocent fanatic.

After questioning the Master, Pilate went back to the chief priests and the accusers of Jesus and said: "I have examined this man, and I find no fault in him. I do not think he is guilty of the charges you have made against him; I think he ought to be set free." And when the Jews heard this, they were moved with great anger, so much so that they wildly shouted that Jesus should die; and one of the Sanhedrists boldly stepped up by the side of Pilate, saying: "This man stirs up the people, beginning in Galilee and continuing throughout all Judea. He is a mischief-maker and an evildoer. You will long regret it if you let this wicked man go free."

Pilate was hard pressed to know what to do with Jesus; therefore, when he heard them say that he began his work in Galilee, he thought to avoid the responsibility of deciding the case, at least to gain time for thought, by sending Jesus to appear before Herod, who was then in the city attending the Passover. Pilate also thought that this gesture would help to antidote some of the bitter feeling which had existed for some time between himself and Herod, due to numerous misunderstandings over matters of jurisdiction.

Pilate, calling the guards, said: "This man is a Galilean. Take him forthwith to Herod, and when he has examined him, report his findings to me." And they took Jesus to Herod.[29]

Jesus Before Herod

When Herod Antipas stopped in Jerusalem, he stayed in the Maccabean palace of Herod the Great, it was here that Jesus was now taken by the temple guards, and he was followed by his accusers and an increasing amount of people. Herod heard about Jesus for some time now and was curious concerning him. When Jesus stood on this Friday morning before the wicked Idumean, not for one moment did he recall Jesus as the lad many years before who had appeared before him in Sepphoris pleading for a just decision in regards to money due his father who had been accidentally killed while at work on one of the public building. As far as Herod was concerned he never saw Jesus before. Herod heard much about Jesus' miracles, and he really hoped he could see him perform some wonder.

When they brought Jesus before this subordinate ruler, he was startled by his stately appearance and the clam composure of his features. For fifteen minutes, he asked Jesus questions, but the Master would not answer him. Herod ridiculed him and dared him to perform a miracle, but, Jesus would not reply to his many inquiries or respond to his heckling.

After interviewing Jesus, Herod listened to the chief priest and Sadducees accusations, he heard all and more than Pilate had listen to regarding the evil doings of Jesus. Finally, after being convinced Jesus won't talk or perform a miracle Herod, after making fun of Jesus for a while, arrayed him in an old purple robe and sent him back to Pilate. Herod knew he had no jurisdiction over Jesus in Judea. Though he believed he was going to finally be rid of Jesus in Galilee, he was thankful it was Pilate who had the responsibility of putting him to death. Herod had never fully recovered from the fear that cursed him as the result of putting John the Baptist to death.

These final moments in the trial of Jesus are so important, I feel it is necessary to quote so that the reader will get the full impact.

"When the guards had brought Jesus back to Pilate, he went out on the front steps of the praetorium, where his judgment seat had been placed, and calling together the chief priests and Sanhedrists, said to them: "You brought this man before me with charges that he perverts the people, forbids the payment of taxes, and claims to be king of the Jews. I have examined him and fail to find him guilty of these charges. In fact, I find no fault in him. Then I sent him to Herod, and the tetrarch must have reached the same conclusion since he has sent him back to us. Certainly, nothing worthy of death has been done by this man. If you still think he needs to be disciplined, I am willing to chastise him before I release him."

Just as the Jews were about to engage in shouting their protests against the release of Jesus, a vast crowd came marching up to the praetorium for the purpose of asking Pilate for the release of a prisoner in honor of the Passover feast. For some time it had been the custom of the Roman governors to allow the populace to choose some imprisoned or condemned man for pardon at the time of the Passover. And now that this crowd had come before him to ask for the release of a prisoner, and since Jesus had so recently been in great favor with the multitudes, it occurred to Pilate that he might possibly extricate himself from his predicament by proposing to this group that, since Jesus was now a prisoner before his judgment seat, he release to them this man of Galilee as the token of Passover good will.

As the crowd surged up on the steps of the building, Pilate heard them calling out the name of one Barabbas. Barabbas was a noted political agitator and murderous robber, the son of a priest, who had recently been apprehended in the act of robbery and murder on the Jericho road. This man was under sentence to die as soon as the Passover festivities were over.

Pilate stood up and explained to the crowd that Jesus had been brought to him by the chief priests, who sought to have him put to death on certain charges, and that he did not think the man was worthy of death. Said Pilate: "Which, therefore, would you prefer that I release to you, this Barabbas, the murderer, or this Jesus of Galilee?" And when Pilate had thus spoken, the chief priests and the Sanhedrin councilors all shouted at the top of their voices, "Barabbas, Barabbas!" And when the people saw that the chief priests were minded to have Jesus put to death, they quickly joined in the clamor for his life while they loudly shouted for the release of Barabbas.

A few days before this the multitude had stood in awe of Jesus, but the mob did not look up to one who, having claimed to be the Son of God, now found himself in the custody of the chief priests and the rulers and on trial before Pilate for his life. Jesus could be a hero in the eyes of the populace when he was driving the money-changers and the traders out of the temple, but not when he was a nonresisting prisoner in the hands of his enemies and on trial for his life.

Pilate was angered at the sight of the chief priests clamoring for the pardon of a notorious murderer while they shouted for the blood of Jesus. He saw their malice and hatred and perceived their prejudice and envy. Therefore he said to them: "How could you choose the life of a murderer in preference to this man's whose worst crime is that he figuratively calls himself the king of the Jews?" But this was not a wise statement for Pilate to make. The Jews were a proud people, now subject to the Roman political yoke but hoping for the coming of a Messiah who would deliver them from gentile bondage with a great show of power and glory. They resented, more than Pilate could know, the intimation that this meekmannered teacher of strange doctrines, now under arrest and charged with crimes worthy of death, should be referred to as "the king of the Jews." They looked upon such a remark as an insult to everything which they held sacred and honorable in their national existence, and therefore did they all let loose their mighty shouts for Barabbas's release and Jesus' death.

Pilate knew Jesus was innocent of the charges brought against him, and had he been a just and courageous judge, he would have acquitted him and turned him loose. But he was afraid to defy these angry Jews, and while he hesitated to do his duty, a messenger came up and presented him with a sealed message from his wife, Claudia.

Pilate indicated to those assembled before him that he wished to read the communication which he had just received before he proceeded further with the matter before him. When Pilate opened this letter from his wife, he read: "I pray you have nothing to do with this innocent and just man whom they call Jesus. I have suffered many things in a dream this night because of him." This note from Claudia not only greatly upset Pilate and thereby delayed the adjudication of this matter, but it unfortunately also provided considerable time in which the Jewish rulers freely circulated among the crowd and urged the people to call for the release of Barabbas and to clamor for the crucifixion of Jesus.

Finally, Pilate addressed himself once more to the solution of the problem which confronted him, by asking the mixed assembly of Jewish rulers and the pardon-seeking crowd, "What shall I do with him who is called the king of the Jews?" And they all shouted with one accord, "Crucify him! Crucify him!" The unanimity of this demand from the mixed multitude startled and alarmed Pilate, the unjust and fear-ridden judge.

Then once more Pilate said: "Why would you crucify this man? What evil has he done? Who will come forward to testify against him?" But when they heard Pilate speak in defense of Jesus, they only cried out all the more, "Crucify him! Crucify him!"

Then again Pilate appealed to them regarding the release of the Passover prisoner, saying: "Once more I ask you, which of these prisoners shall I release to you at this, your Passover time?" And again the crowd shouted, "Give us Barabbas!"

Then said Pilate: "If I release the murderer, Barabbas, what shall I do with Jesus?" And once more the multitude shouted in unison, "Crucify him! Crucify him!"

Pilate was terrorized by the insistent clamor of the mob, acting under the direct leadership of the chief priests and the councilors of the Sanhedrin; nevertheless, he decided upon at least one more attempt to appease the crowd and save Jesus.[30]

Pilate's Last Appeal

"In all that is transpiring early this Friday morning before Pilate, only the enemies of Jesus are participating. His many friends either do not yet know of his night arrest and early morning trial or are in hiding lest they also be apprehended and adjudged worthy of death because they

believe Jesus' teachings. In the multitude which now clamors for the Master's death are to be found only his sworn enemies and the easily led and unthinking populace.

Pilate would make one last appeal to their pity. Being afraid to defy the clamor of this misled mob who cried for the blood of Jesus, he ordered the Jewish guards and the Roman soldiers to take Jesus and scourge him. This was in itself an unjust and illegal procedure since the Roman law provided that only those condemned to die by crucifixion should be thus subjected to scourging. The guards took Jesus into the open courtyard of the praetorium for this ordeal. Though his enemies did not witness this scourging, Pilate did, and before they had finished this wicked abuse, he directed the scourgers to desist and indicated that Jesus should be brought to him. Before the scourgers laid their knotted whips upon Jesus as he was bound to the whipping post, they again put upon him the purple robe, and plaiting a crown of thorns, they placed it upon his brow. And when they had put a reed in his hand as a mock scepter, they knelt before him and mocked him, saying, "Hail, king of the Jews!" And they spit upon him and struck him in the face with their hands. And one of them, before they returned him to Pilate, took the reed from his hand and struck him upon the head.

Then Pilate led forth this bleeding and lacerated prisoner and, presenting him before the mixed multitude, said: "Behold the man! Again I declare to you that I find no crime in him, and having scourged him, I would release him."

There stood Jesus of Nazareth, clothed in an old purple royal robe with a crown of thorns piercing his kindly brow. His face was bloodstained and his form bowed down with suffering and grief. But nothing can appeal to the unfeeling hearts of those who are victims of intense emotional hatred and slaves to religious prejudice. This sight sent a mighty shudder through the realms of a vast universe, but it did not touch the hearts of those who had set their minds to effect the destruction of Jesus.

When they had recovered from the first shock of seeing the Master's plight, they only shouted the louder and the longer, "Crucify him! Crucify him! Crucify him!"

And now did Pilate comprehend that it was futile to appeal to their supposed feelings of pity. He stepped forward and said: "I perceive that you are determined this man shall die, but what has he done to deserve death? Who will declare his crime?"

Then the high priest himself stepped forward and, going up to Pilate, angrily declared: "We have a sacred law, and by that law this man ought to die because he made himself out to be the Son of God." When Pilate heard this, he was all the more afraid, not only of the Jews, but recalling his wife's note and the Greek mythology of the gods coming down on earth, he now trembled at the thought of Jesus possibly being a divine personage. He waved to the crowd to hold its peace while he took Jesus by the arm and again led him inside the building that he might further examine him. Pilate was now confused by fear, bewildered by superstition, and harassed by the stubborn attitude of the mob."[31]

Pilate's Last Interview

As Pilate, trembling with fearful emotion, sat down by the side of Jesus, he inquired: "Where do you come from? Really, who are you? What is this they say, that you are the Son of God?"

But Jesus could hardly answer such questions when asked by a man-fearing, weak, and vacillating judge who was so unjust as to subject him to flogging even when he had declared him innocent of all crime, and before he had been duly sentenced to die. Jesus looked Pilate straight in the face, but he did not answer him. Then said Pilate: "Do you refuse to speak to me? Do you not realize that I still have power to release you or to crucify you?" Then said Jesus: "You could have no power over me except it were permitted from above. You could exercise no authority over the Son of Man unless the Father in heaven allowed it. But you are not so guilty since you are ignorant of the gospel. He who betrayed me and he who delivered me to you, they have the greater sin."

This last talk with Jesus thoroughly frightened Pilate. This moral coward and judicial weakling now labored under the double weight of the superstitious fear of Jesus and mortal dread of the Jewish leaders.

Again Pilate appeared before the crowd, saying: "I am certain this man is only a religious offender. You should take him and judge him by your law. Why should you expect that I would consent to his death because he has clashed with your traditions?"

Pilate was just about ready to release Jesus when Caiaphas, the high priest, approached the cowardly Roman judge and, shaking an avenging finger in Pilate's face, said with angry words which the entire multitude could hear: "If you release this man, you are not Caesar's friend, and I will see that the emperor knows all." This public threat was too much for Pilate. Fear for his personal fortunes now eclipsed all other considerations, and the cowardly governor ordered Jesus brought out before the judgment seat. As the Master stood there before them, he pointed to him and tauntingly said, "Behold your king." And the Jews answered, "Away with him. Crucify him!" And then Pilate said, with much irony and sarcasm, "Shall I crucify your king?" And the Jews answered, "Yes, crucify him! We have no king but Caesar." And then did Pilate realize that there was no hope of saving Jesus since he was unwilling to defy the Jews.[32]

Pilate Tragic Surrender

Here stood the Son of God incarnate as the Son of Man. He was arrested without indictment; accused without evidence; adjudged without witnesses; punished without a verdict; and now was soon to be condemned to die by an unjust judge who confessed that he could find no fault in him. If Pilate had thought to appeal to their patriotism by referring to Jesus as the "king of the Jews," he utterly failed. The Jews were not expecting any such a king. The declaration of the chief priests and the Sadducees, "We have no king but Caesar," was a shock even to the unthinking populace, but it was too late now to save Jesus even had the mob dared to espouse the Master's cause.

Pilate was afraid of a tumult or a riot. He dared not risk having such a disturbance during Passover time in Jerusalem. He had recently received a reprimand from Caesar, and he would not risk another. The mob cheered when he ordered the release of Barabbas. Then he ordered a basin and some water, and there before the multitude he washed his hands, saying: "I am innocent of the blood of this man. You are determined that he shall die, but I have found no guilt in him. See you to it. The soldiers will lead him forth." And then the mob cheered and replied, "His blood be on us and on our children."[33]

Just Before the Crucifixion

As Jesus and his accuser started off to see Herod, the Master turned to the apostle John and said: *"John you can do no more for me. Go to my mother and bring her to me ere I die."*[34] When John heard his Master's request, he was reluctant to leave Jesus alone with his enemies, but he hurry off to Bethany were the entire family was assemble in waiting at the home of Martha and Mary, the sister of Lazarus whom Jesus raised from the dead.

Several times during the morning of Jesus' trial the messenger of David Zebedee brought news of the progress of Jesus' trial. The family of Jesus didn't reach Bethany until just a few minutes before the arrival of John with the request of Jesus to see his mother before he was put to death. After John Zebedee told them all that had happen since the arrest of Jesus at midnight, Mary, his mother, went at once in the company of John to see her oldest son. By the time Mary and John reached the city, Jesus, along with the Roman soldiers, had already reached Golgotha.

When Mary, the mother of Jesus, started out to see her son, his sister Ruth refused to remain behind with the rest of the family. She was determined to go with her mother. Her brother Jude went with her. The rest of Jesus' family remained in Bethany under the direction of James, one of Jesus' apostle, and almost every hour, a messenger of David Zebedee brought reports of the progress of the terrible time of putting to death their oldest brother, Jesus of Nazareth.

The End of Judas Iscariot

"It was about half past eight o'clock this Friday morning when the hearing of Jesus before Pilate was ended and the Master was placed in the custody of the Roman soldiers who were to crucify him. As soon as the Romans took possession of Jesus, the captain of the Jewish guards marched with his men back to their temple headquarters. The chief priest and his Sanhedrist associates followed close behind the guards, going directly to their usual meeting place in the hall of hewn stone in the temple. Here they found many other members of the Sanhedrin waiting to learn what had been done with Jesus. As Caiaphas was engaged in making his report to the Sanhedrin regarding the trial and condemnation of Jesus, Judas appeared before them to claim his reward for the part he had played in his Master's arrest and sentence of death.

All of these Jews loathed Judas; they looked upon the betrayer with only feelings of utter contempt. Throughout the trial of Jesus before Caiaphas and during his appearance before Pilate, Judas was pricked in his conscience about his traitorous conduct. And he was also beginning to become somewhat disillusioned regarding the reward he was to receive as payment for his services as Jesus' betrayer. He did not like the coolness and aloofness of the Jewish authorities; nevertheless, he expected to be liberally rewarded for his cowardly conduct. He anticipated being called before the full meeting of the Sanhedrin and there hearing himself eulogized while they conferred upon him suitable honors in token of the great service which he flattered himself he had rendered his nation. Imagine, therefore, the great surprise of this egotistic traitor when a servant of the high priest, tapping him on the shoulder, called him just outside the hall and said: "Judas, I have been appointed to pay you for the betrayal of Jesus. Here is your reward." And thus speaking, the servant of Caiaphas handed Judas a bag containing thirty pieces of silver — the current price of a good, healthy slave.

Judas was stunned, dumfounded. He rushed back to enter the hall but was debarred by the doorkeeper. He wanted to appeal to the Sanhedrin, but they would not admit him. Judas could not believe that these rulers of the Jews would allow him to betray his friends and his Master and then offer him as a reward thirty pieces of silver. He was humiliated, disillusioned, and utterly crushed. He walked away from the temple, as it were, in a trance. He automatically dropped the money bag in his deep pocket, that same pocket wherein he had so long carried the bag containing the apostolic funds. And he wandered out through the city after the crowds who were on their way to witness the crucifixions.

From a distance Judas saw them raise the cross piece with Jesus nailed thereon, and upon sight of this he rushed back to the temple and, forcing his way past the doorkeeper, found himself standing in the presence of the Sanhedrin, which was still in session. The betrayer was well-nigh breathless and highly distraught, but he managed to stammer out these words: "I have sinned in that I have betrayed innocent blood. You have insulted me. You have offered me as a reward for my service, money — the price of a slave. I repent that I have done this; here is your money. I want to escape the guilt of this deed."

When the rulers of the Jews heard Judas, they scoffed at him. One of them sitting near where Judas stood, motioned that he should leave the hall and said: "Your Master has already been put to death by the Romans, and as for your guilt, what is that to us? See you to that — and begone!"

As Judas left the Sanhedrin chamber, he removed the thirty pieces of silver from the bag and threw them broadcast over the temple floor. When the betrayer left the temple, he was almost beside himself. Judas was now passing through the experience of the realization of the true nature of sin. All the glamour, fascination, and intoxication of wrongdoing had vanished. Now the evildoer stood alone and face to face with the judgment verdict of his disillusioned and disappointed soul. Sin was bewitching and adventurous in the committing, but now must the harvest of the naked and unromantic facts be faced.

This onetime ambassador of the kingdom of heaven on earth now walked through the streets of Jerusalem, forsaken and alone. His despair was desperate and well-nigh absolute. On his journeyed through the city and outside the walls, on down into the terrible solitude of the valley of Hinnom, where he climbed up the steep rocks and, taking the girdle of his cloak, fastened one end to a small tree, tied the other about his neck, and cast himself over the precipice. Ere he was dead, the knot which his nervous hands had tied gave way, and the betrayer's body was dashed to pieces as it fell on the jagged rocks below."[35]

CHAPTER 7

The Burial of Jesus

Before ending this book, I want to bring out one of the main purposes for Jesus' mission on our planet that the so called religions of authority, as Jesus so accurately called them (human authority), overlooked for so many years.

Jesus stayed on the cross about an hour after his death. They would have taken him down sooner, but they were waiting for the dispatching of a military unit.

The rulers of the Jews planned on throwing Jesus' body in the open burial pits of Gehenna, in the south part of the city. It was the custom to dispose of bodies of victims of crucifixion. If those Jewish leaders had their way, Jesus body would have been exposed to the wild animals.

Joseph of Arimathea along with Nicodemus had gone to plead with Pilate for the body of Jesus to be turned over to them for the proper burial. Often, friends of a person crucified would offer bribes to the Roman authorities to get possession of the body of their interest. Joseph went to Pilate with a large sum of money in case he needed it to pay for permission to remove Jesus' body to a private burial tomb. Pilate would not take any money for this. When he learned of Joseph and Nicodemus's request, he quickly signed the order, which authorized Joseph to go to Golgotha and immediately take full possession of the Master's body. In the meantime, a group of Jews representing the Sanhedrin had gone out to Golgotha to make sure that Jesus' body was with the soldiers when they went to the public burial pits.

When Joseph and Nicodemus reached Golgotha with their order, they found the soldiers were taking Jesus' body down from the cross, and those that represented the Sanhedrin (the highest judicial and ecclesiastical council of the ancient Jewish nation) stood by to make sure his body was taken to the criminal burial pit. When Joseph presented Pilate's order for the Master's body to the centurion, the Jews raised hell; as they raved, they sought violently to take possession of the body, and when they did this, the centurion ordered four of his soldiers to his side and with drawn swords, they stood astride the Master's body as it lay there on the ground. The centurion ordered the other soldiers to leave the bodies of the two thieves while they drove back this angry mob of infuriated Jews. After order was restored, the centurion read the order from Pilate to the Jews, and he stepped aside and said to Joseph, "This body is yours to do with it as you see· fit. I and my soldiers will stand by to see that no man interferes," *The Urantia Book.*

Crucified bodies were not allowed to be buried in Jewish cemetery: there was a strict law against it. Joseph and Nicodemus knew this law so they decided to bury Jesus in Joseph's new family tomb hewn out of solid rock; it was located a short distance north of where Jesus was crucified, and across the road leading to Samaria. No one had ever lain in this tomb and they thought it appropriate that the Master should rest there. Joseph sincerely believed that Jesus would rise from the dead, but Nicodemus was skeptical. Joseph and Nicodemus were formal members of the Sanhedrin; they kept their faith in Jesus a secret from their fellow Sanhedrists for a long time some member suspected them even before they withdrew from the council. From that time on they were the most outspoken disciples in all Jerusalem.

Around four-thirty that Friday afternoon, the burial procession for Jesus of Nazareth started from Golgotha to Joseph's tomb across the way. The body was wrapped in a linen sheet as four men carried it, followed by those faithful women of Jesus' group from Galilee. The men that carried the body of Jesus to the tomb were: Joseph, Nicodemus, John, and the Roman centurion.

They carried the body into the tomb a chamber about ten feet squared, where they rushed to prepare it for burial. The Jew's did not bury their dead; they embalmed them. Joseph and Nicodemus had brought with them a large amount of myrrh and aloes; they wrapped the body with bandage and saturated it with solution they had brought with them. When the embalming was finished, they tied napkins around his face, wrapped his body in a linen sheet and reverently placed it on a shelf in the tomb. After the body was completed and placed, the centurion had his soldiers to place the door-stone before the entrance of the tomb. The soldiers then took the body of the thieves to Gehenna, while the others went off to Jerusalem in sorrow to observe the Passover according to the laws of Moses.

The men that prepared Jesus for burial were in a considerable hurry because this was the preparation day and the Sabbath was drawing near. The men hurried back to the city, while the women lingered by the tomb until it was very dark.

While all of the above was going on, the women were hiding nearby, so they saw all that took place; they saw where they laid the Master's body. They hid themselves because it was not permissible for women to be with men at this time according to the Jewish law. The women that lingered behind did not think Jesus body was properly prepared for the burial rest; they reached the conclusion that they would go back to the home of Joseph, rest over the Sabbath, then prepare spices and ointment and return on Sunday morning and properly prepare the Master's body for the death rest. The women that stayed at the tomb Friday evening were: Mary Magdalene, the wife of Clopas, Martha another sister of Jesus' mother, and Rebecca of Sepphoris, the woman that wanted to marry Jesus when he was around nineteen.

Other than David Zebedee and Joseph of Arimathea, very few of Jesus' disciples believed or understood that Jesus was due to rise from the tomb on the third-day.

The Real Jesus

If Jesus followers were not mindful that Jesus had promised to rise up from the grave on the third-day, his enemies were. The chief priest, Pharisees and Sadducees remembered; they had received the report that if his life was taken in three-days, he would rise from the dead. That Friday night, after the Passover Supper, around midnight, a group of Jewish leaders gathered at the home of Caiaphas, where they talked about their fear of Jesus claiming that on the third-day after his death, he would rise up from the dead. The meeting ended with them coming to an agreement that a group of Sanhedrims would visit Pilate early the next day with the official request of the Sanhedrin that Romans guard be placed at Jesus' tomb to prevent his friends from tampering with it. The Sanhedrin spokesman of this committee said to Pilate: *"Sir we remember that this deceiver, Jesus of Nazareth, said while he were yet alive, after three-days I will raise again. Therefore, we come to you with the request that you issue guards that would make sure his sepulcher is secured against his followers, at least until after the third-day. We fear that his disciples will come and steal him during the night, and then claim to the people that he has risen from the dead. If this was allowed to happen, this mistake would be far worse than allowing him to live.* [1]

When Pilate heard the request of the Sanhedrims, he said: *"I will give a guard of ten soldiers, go your way and make the tomb secure."* The Sanhedrims went back to their temple and secured ten of their own guards, and then marched out to Joseph's tomb with ten of their guards and ten of the Roman soldiers on the Sabbath morning to watch over Jesus' tomb. These men rolled another stone in front of the tomb, and set the seal of palate on and around these stones, in case they were disturbed without their knowledge. And these twenty remained on watch up to the hour of the resurrection; the Jews carried them their food and drinks.

All throughout the Sabbath day, the disciples and apostles were in hiding while the whole of Jerusalem discussed the death of Jesus on the cross. There were about one and a half-million Jews present in Jerusalem at that time, coming from all parts of the Roman Empire and from Mesopotamia. This was the start of the Passover week; all of these pilgrims were in the city and learned of the resurrection of Jesus. They'd carry the news back home with them.

Late that Saturday night, John Mark called a meeting for the eleven apostles to meet secretly at his father's home; just before midnight, they all assembled in the same upper chamber where they had their last supper with Jesus two nights before.

Mary, the mother of Jesus, along with Ruth and Jude, all returned to Bethany to be with their family this Saturday evening, just prior to sunset. David Zebedee stayed at the home of Nicodemus; he had arranged for his messengers to gather early Sunday morning. The women of Galilee stayed at the home of Joseph of Arimathea. Here is a quote from *The Urantia Book* on the meaning of the death on the cross.

Meaning of the Death on the Cross

Although Jesus did not die this death on the cross to atone for the racial guilt of mortal man nor to provide some sort of effective approach to an otherwise offended and unforgiving God; even though the Son of Man did not offer himself as a sacrifice to appease the wrath of God and to open the way for sinful man to obtain salvation; notwithstanding that these ideas of atonement and propitiation are erroneous, nonetheless, there are significances attached to this death of Jesus on the cross which should not be overlooked. It is a fact that Urantia has become known among other neighboring inhabited planets as the "World of the Cross."

Jesus desired to live a full mortal life in the flesh on Urantia. Death is, ordinarily, a part of life. Death is the last act in the mortal drama. In your well-meant efforts to escape the superstitious errors of the false interpretation of the meaning of the death on the cross, you should be careful not to make the great mistake of failing to perceive the true significance and the genuine import of the Master's death.

Mortal man was never the property of the archdeceivers. Jesus did not die to ransom man from the clutch of the apostate rulers and fallen princes of the spheres. The Father in heaven never conceived of such crass injustice as damning a mortal soul because of the evil-doing of his ancestors. Neither was the Master's death on the cross a sacrifice which consisted in an effort to pay God a debt which the race of mankind had come to owe him.

Before Jesus lived on earth, you might possibly have been justified in believing in such a God, but not since the Master lived and died among your fellow mortals. Moses taught the dignity and justice of a Creator God; but Jesus portrayed the love and mercy of a heavenly Father.

The animal nature — the tendency toward evil-doing — may be hereditary, but sin is not transmitted from parent to child. Sin is the act of conscious and deliberate rebellion against the Father's will and the Sons' laws by an individual will creature.

Jesus lived and died for a whole universe, not just for the races of this one world. While the mortals of the realms had salvation even before Jesus lived and died on Urantia, it is nevertheless a fact that his bestowal on this world greatly illuminated the way of salvation; his death did much to make forever plain the certainty of mortal survival after death in the flesh.

Though it is hardly proper to speak of Jesus as a sacrificer, a ransomer, or a redeemer, it is wholly correct to refer to him as a savior. He forever made the way of salvation (survival) more clear and certain; he did better and more surely showed the way of salvation for all the mortals of all the worlds of the universe of Nebadon.

When once you grasp the idea of God as a true and loving Father, the only concept which Jesus ever taught, you must forthwith, in all consistency, utterly abandon all those primitive notions about God as an offended monarch, a stern and all-powerful ruler whose chief delight is to detect his subjects in wrongdoing and to see that they are adequately punished, unless some being almost equal to himself should volunteer to suffer for them, to die as a substitute and in their stead. The whole idea of ransom and atonement is incompatible with the concept of God as it was taught and exemplified by Jesus of Nazareth. The infinite love of God is not secondary to anything in the divine nature.

All this concept of atonement and sacrificial salvation is rooted and grounded in selfishness. Jesus taught that service to one's fellows is the highest concept of the brotherhood of spirit believers. Salvation should be taken for granted by those who believe in the fatherhood of God. The believer's chief concern should not be the selfish desire for personal salvation but rather the unselfish urge to love and, therefore, serve one's fellows even as Jesus loved and served mortal men.

Neither do genuine believers trouble themselves so much about the future punishment of sin. The real believer is only concerned about present separation from God. True, wise fathers may chasten their sons, but they do all this in love and for corrective purposes. They do not punish in anger, neither do they chastise in retribution.

Even if God were the stern and legal monarch of a universe in which justice ruled supreme, he certainly would not be satisfied with the childish scheme of substituting an innocent sufferer for a guilty offender.

The great thing about the death of Jesus, as it is related to the enrichment of human experience and the enlargement of the way of salvation, is not the fact of his death, but rather the superb manner and the matchless spirit in which he met death.

This entire idea of the ransom of the atonement places salvation upon a plane of unreality; such a concept is purely philosophic. Human salvation is real; it is based on two realities which may be grasped by the creature's faith and thereby become incorporated into individual human experience: the fact of the fatherhood of God and its correlated truth, the brotherhood of man. It is true, after all that you are to be "forgiven your debts, even as you forgive your debtors. "[2]

Jesus died to prove to mortal man that we will continue to live if we follow in His footsteps. Those that don't live by the law of life will go to the second death mentioned in (Revelation 2:11) *"He that hath an ear, let him hear what the spirit saith unto the churches; he that overcometh shall not be hurt of the second death."*

The Morontia Transit

Morontia is the stuff the lower parts of the spiritual dimension are made of including the soul—according to those Higher Beings. We mortals, have to come to the realization that as Jesus' body lay in Joseph's tomb, there was a great deal of activity going on in this Morontia dimension that we are not able to see into at this stage of our evolution perhaps in the distance future, some of us may be able to do so. However, the being that presented these papers had this to say about the goings on in that dimension at the time Jesus' body laid in the tomb.

The midwayer stated that at two-forty-five Sunday morning, the Paradise Incarnation Commission consisting of seven unidentified Paradise personalities arrived on the scene where Jesus' body rested; right away, they dispersed themselves about the tomb (Paradise is the ultimate heaven). At ten minutes before three, forceful vibrations of mingling material and Morontia activities began to come from Joseph's tomb, and at two minutes past three o'clock that

Sunday morning, April 9, A.D. 30, the resurrected Morontia form and personality of Jesus of Nazareth came forth from the tomb.

After the resurrected spiritual body of Jesus came forth from the burial tomb, the body of flesh in which he lived and worked for almost thirty-six years still laying there in the sepulcher undisturbed in any way; the seal of Pilate was still intact; the soldiers were yet on guard. The temple guards were on continuous duty; the Roman guards were changed at midnight. None of these so called keepers that were watching over the tomb suspected that the one they were watching over was now a discarded form that had no further connection with the resurrected Morontia personality of Jesus. This is the most important reason Jesus allowed himself to die on the cross: to prove to us that life is a continuum. This is an important fact that the Western world has been ignoring for two-thousand years. They replaced it with the sacrificial lamb that has no meaning in the spiritual world whatsoever.

After Jesus' resurrection, the chief archangels of the resurrection approached Gabriel and asked for the body of Jesus, and he said, *"We may not participate in the Morontia resurrection of the bestowal experience of Michael (Jesus) our sovereign but we would have his mortal remains put in our custody for immediate dissolution. We do not propose to employ our technique of dematerialization; we merely wish to invoke the process of the acceleration of time. It is enough that we have seen the sovereign live and die on Urantia; the hosts of heaven would be spared the memory of enduring the sight of slow decay of the human form of the Creator and upholder of a universe. In the name of the celestial intelligences of all of Nebadon, I ask for a mandate giving me the custody of the mortal body of Jesus of Nazareth and empowering us to proceed with its immediate dissolution."*[3]

After Gabriel, granted the chief archangel, his request, he summoned numerous hosts of all orders of celestial

The Real Jesus

personalities, and then with the help of the midwayers, proceeded to take possession of Jesus' physical body. The dead body of Jesus was a physical, material body; it could not be removed out of the tomb as the Morontia resurrection body of Jesus had been. As they got ready to move the body from the tomb for its disposal of near instantaneous dissolution, it was assigned to the midwayers to roll the stones from the entrance of the tomb. The larger of these two stone was a huge circular stone a lot like a millstone, and it moved in a grove chiseled out of the rock so that it could be rolled back and forth to open and close the tomb.

When the watching Jewish guards and the Roman soldiers saw the huge stone moving away from the entrance of the tomb in the dim light of the morning, apparently by no visible means, their fear overwhelmed them; they panicked, made haste and fled. The Jewish guards fled to their homes; after a while, they went to the temple and told all of what had happened. The Roman soldiers fled to the fortress of Antonia and reported what they had seen to the centurion as soon as he came on duty.

The hypocritical Jewish leaders tried to get rid of Jesus by bribing the traitorous Judas, and now they are embarrassed with a perplexed situation; instead of thinking of punishing the guards for leaving their post, they resorted to bribing these guards and the Roman soldiers. They paid off each of these twenty men with a certain sum of money. And they gave them orders to tell people that while they slept during the night, Jesus' disciples slipped among them and took the body away. Those Jewish leaders made a solemn promise to the soldiers that if Pilate found out what had happened, they would defend them.

The Christian belief of the resurrection is based on the fact that the tomb Jesus laid in was empty; this was a fact, but this is not the truth about the resurrection; no one at that time ever imagined what was really going on behind the scenes. Because Jesus' body was not there when the first believers arrived, they assumed the physical body had resurrected. The body was not there because the celestials had been granted their request to take the body of Jesus for its special and unique dissolution, it returned to the dust from whence it came. Even in the Christian *Bible,* it states that flesh and blood cannot inherit the kingdom 1 Corinthians 15:50. The mortal remains of Jesus went through the same natural process of elemental disintegration as all other human bodies only the process as far as Jesus' body was concerned, was greatly accelerated to the point that it was almost instantaneous. There were almost one thousand people that saw Jesus in his Morontia body. There is no doubt that those who saw Jesus in his higher body remained in a state of awesome wonder for the rest of their lives.

Although there are seven hundred pages on the life and teachings of Jesus in *The Urantia Book,* I tried to give some of the most important aspects, hoping the reader will grasp the purpose of Jesus, sojourn on our planet. After reading my work you must decide for yourself if you want to continue and read *The Urantia Book,* and learn more. I am a seeker at heart.

GLOSSARY

Andon—the first male human being killed during an earth earthquake at age 42.

Caligastia—Served as planetary Prince of Earth until he betrayed his trust and joined Lucifer rebellion approximately 200,000 years ago.

Fonta—the first female human being killed during an earthquake at age 42.

Melchizedek—is an order of Higher Beings; there are about ten million in our local Universe. They are dispatched to worlds that have need of them.

One of them visited our world during the time of Abraham; in the higher Worlds, he is known as Machiventa.

Midwayers—creatures that appear on most inhabited worlds; they exist and function in the realm "midway" between humans and angels.

Morontia—that phase of universe reality between the material and the spiritual realms.

Nebadon—the name of our local universe.

Nodites—descendents of the rebel member of Caligastia (the prince of this world) corporeal staff that later built the land of Nod in the *Bible*. They are called Son of God in the *Bible,* Genesis 6:4. See my book, *Journey to Life*.

Salvington—Salvington, headquarters of our local Universe, Nabadon, which is governed by our Creator Son Christ Michael with his Mother Spirit consort.

Satan—A high assistant of Lucifer

Satania—the administrative system of approximately 1,000 inhabitable planets to which our earth belong.

Introduction

[1] All Quotes pertaining to the *Bible* are taken from The Scofield Reference Bible, Oxford University Press 1937.

Chapter 1

[1] *The Urantia Book* page 1321, The Urantia Foundation.
[2] *The Urantia Book* paper 120, page 1323, The Urantia Foundation.
[3] *The Urantia Book* paper 120, page 1329, section 3 The Urantia Foundation.
[4] *The Urantia Book* page 1343, acknowledgement paragraph 1, The Urantia Foundation.
[5] *The Urantia Book* page 1347, section 4, paragraph 1, The Urantia Foundation.
[6] *The Urantia Book* page 1352, paragraph 3, The Urantia Foundation.
[7] *The Urantia Book,* page 1353, The Urantia Foundation.
[8] *The Urantia Book,* page 1361, paragraph 7, The Urantia Foundation.

Chapter 2

[1] *The Urantia Book,* Page 1378, paragraph 1, The Urantia Foundation.
[2] *The Urantia Book*, Page 1387, paragraph 1, The Urantia Foundation.

Chapter 3

[1] *The Urantia Book* page 1390, and paragraph 3, The Urantia Foundation.
[2] *The Urantia Book* page 1397, paragraph 4, 5, and 6 The Urantia Foundation.
[3] *The Urantia Book* page 1421 section 3 paragraph 4, The Urantia Foundation.
[4] *The Urantia Book,* Page 1428, middle of paragraph 2. The Urantia Foundation 1955.
[5] *The Urantia Book* page 1431, paragraph 3, The Urantia Foundation.
[6] *The Urantia Book* page 1494, paragraph 2, The Urantia Foundation 1955.

Chapter 4

[1] The Urantia Book page 1504, paragraph 5, section 8, The Urantia Foundation 1955.
[2] The Urantia Book page 1505, paragraph 4, section 9, The Urantia Foundation 1955.
[3] The Urantia Book page 1525, paragraph 3, section 1, The Urantia Foundation 1955.

Chapter 5

[1] *The Urantia Book* page 1529, paragraph 5 and 1530 paragraph 1-3, The Urantia Foundation 1955
[2] *The Urantia Book* page 1597, section 2 paragraph 1. The Urantia Foundation 1955.
[3] *The Urantia Book* page 1661, starting at section 5, The Urantia Foundation.
[4] *Journey to Life,* 2011 Infinity Publishing.
[5] *The Urantia Book* page 1729, paragraph 1, The Urantia Foundation 1955.
[6] *The Urantia Book* page 1846, paragraph 1, The Urantia Foundation 1955.
[7] *The Urantia Book* page 1846, starting at paragraph 6-9, The Urantia Foundation 1955.

Chapter 6

[1] *The Urantia Book* page 1921 paragraph 2, section 1 The Urantia Foundation 1955.
[2] *The Urantia Book* page 1921 paragraphs 1-4, section 2, The Urantia Foundation 1955.
[3] *The Urantia Book* page 1931 paragraphs 15, section 1, The Urantia Foundation 1955.
[4] *The Urantia Book* page 1932 paragraph 1, section 2, The Urantia Foundation 1955.
[5] *The Urantia Book* page 1933 paragraph 4, section 2, The Urantia Foundation 1955.
[6] *The Urantia Book* page 1933 paragraph 5, section 2, The Urantia

Foundation 1955.

[7] *The Urantia Book* page 1934 paragraph 2, section 3, The Urantia Foundation 1955.

[8] *The Urantia Book* page 1937 paragraph 1, section 2, The Urantia Foundation 1955.

[9] *The Urantia Book* page 1938 paragraph 2, section 2, The Urantia Foundation 1955.

[10] *The Urantia Book* page 1939 paragraph 3, section 3, The Urantia Foundation 1955.

[11] *The Urantia Book* page 1939 paragraph 5, section 3, The Urantia Foundation 1955

[12] *The Urantia Book* page 1940 paragraph 8, section 3, The Urantia Foundation 1955

[13] *The Urantia Book* page 1940 paragraph 9, section 3, The Urantia Foundation 1955

[14] *The Urantia Book* page 1940 paragraph 1-2, section 4, The Urantia Foundation 1955

[15] *The Urantia Book* page 1941 paragraph 6, section 4, The Urantia Foundation 1955

[16] *The Urantia Book* page 1941-42 paragraph 1-2, section 5, The Urantia Foundation 1955

[17] *The Urantia Book* page 1963 thru 1965 paragraph 1thru 6, section 1, The Urantia Foundation 1955

[18] *The Urantia Book* page 1968 paragraph 1, section 1, The Urantia Foundation 1955

[19] *The Urantia Book* page 1968 paragraph 2 thru 4, section 3, The Urantia Foundation 1955

[20] *The Urantia Book* page 1971 thru 72, paragraph 1 thru 2, section 1, The Urantia Foundation 1955

[21] *The Urantia Book* page 1974, paragraph 4, section 3, The Urantia Foundation 1955

[22] *The Urantia Book* page 1972, paragraph 5, section 3, The Urantia Foundation 1955

[23] *The Urantia Book* page 1974, paragraph 6, section 3, The Urantia Foundation 1955

[24] *The Urantia Book* page 1975, paragraph 7, section 3, The Urantia Foundation 1955

[25] *The Urantia Book* page 1978 thru 1980, paragraph 2 thru 9, section 1, The Urantia Foundation 1955

[26] *The Urantia Book* page1982 to1984, paragraph 6, thru 19, section 3, The Urantia Foundation 1955

[27] *The Urantia Book* page1985 to1986, paragraph 2, thru 11, section 5, The Urantia Foundation 1955
[28] *The Urantia Book* page1990, paragraph 1thru 3, section 2, The Urantia Foundation 1955
[29] *The Urantia Book* page1992, section 3, The Urantia Foundation 1955
[30] *The Urantia Book* page1993 thru 1994, paragraph 1, thru 13, section 5, The Urantia Foundation 1955
[31] *The Urantia Book* page1994 thru 1995, paragraph 1, thru 7, section 6, The Urantia Foundation 1955
[32] *The Urantia Book* page1995-1996, section 7, The Urantia Foundation 1955
[33] *The Urantia Book* page 1996, section 8, The Urantia Foundation 1955
[34] *The Urantia Book* page 1997, paragraph 1, The Urantia Foundation 1955
[35] *The Urantia Book* page 1997, paragraph 1, The Urantia Foundation 1955

Chapter 7

[1] *The Urantia Book* page 2014, section 2, The Urantia Foundation 1955.
[2] *The Urantia Book* page 2016-2017, section 4, paragraph 1-12, The Urantia Foundation 1955.
[3] *The Urantia Book* page 2022, section 2, paragraph 1, The Urantia Foundation 1955.